GOOD THINKING

EDUCATION FOR CITIZENSHIP AND MORAL RESPONSIBILITY

VOLUME 1 **KS3**

TED HUDDLESTON
&
DON ROWE

EVANS
EDUCATION

CITIZENSHIP
FOUNDATION

Published by Evans Brothers Limited
2A Portman Mansions
Chiltern Street
London WiM 1LE

First published 2000

© in the text Citizenship Foundation 2001
© in the illustrations Evans Brothers Limited 2001

Designed and illustrated by Pumpkin House (www.pumpkinhouse.co.uk)

British Library Cataloguing in Publication Data
Huddleston, Ted
    Good thinking
    Vol. 1
    1. Citizenship - Study and teaching (Secondary) - Great Britain
    I. Title II. Rowe, Don, 1946-
    373'.011'5
ISBN 0 237 52165 2

Printed in the UK by Ebenezer Baylis and Son Ltd.

All rights reserved. No part of this publication may be reproduced, stored in a retrieval system or
transmitted in any form or by any means, electronic, mechanical, photocopying, recording or otherwise,
without prior permission of Evans Brothers Limited.

Copyright notice

This book is protected by international copyright law and cannot be copied in any way until it
has been purchased. Teachers are free to reproduce these pages by any method without infringing
copyright restrictions, provided that the number of copies reproduced does not exceed the amount
required in the school of purchase.

CONTENTS

INTRODUCTION

ABOUT THIS BOOK

This book is designed to help pupils learn how to *study, reflect upon and discuss issues of moral concern.*

It is one of three volumes in the *Good Thinking* series. The materials for this series were developed in the course of the Citizenship Foundation's Moral Education in Secondary Schools Project and trialled in over forty secondary schools up and down the country.

These books are intended primarily for use by teachers of Citizenship Education, but also have application in RE, English and General Studies lessons, as well as courses in critical thinking and key skills. In particular, they are designed to support the delivery of the moral component of the programmes of study for citizenship prescribed in the revised national curriculum.

The books are structured according to the 'spiral curriculum' principle, with key concepts such as justice, duty and rights revisited with increasing complexity in successive volumes. Each volume targets a different key stage - 3, 4 and 5, respectively - though, in practice, a certain amount of flexibility is possible with regard to target audience.

The series does not set out to be another *ad hoc* compilation of factual information and well-rehearsed arguments on controversial moral issues of our time, such as abortion, euthanasia or capital punishment. Rather it is a systematic introduction to the kind of basic *skills, knowledge and understanding which make moral argument and debate possible.*

This sort of approach to moral education is very much in its infancy in schools, and teachers may not be familiar with all of the ideas and techniques it involves. For this reason we have included an introduction outlining the nature of the subject-matter and some of the teaching strategies which make for effective learning in the classroom.

The *Good Thinking* materials in this volume are divided into 14 separate topics, or teaching units. Each unit focuses on a different aspect of moral thinking or argument, and contains sufficient material for a lesson's work. Units are set out in the form of outline lesson plans, comprising:

- aims and objectives;
- suggestions for learning activities;
- key questions for discussion and a range of potential responses;
- useful words and phrases;
- further areas for exploration;
- photocopiable student material.

USEFUL WORDS

Language learning is an important aspect of this work, and teachers should try to make use of available opportunities to introduce pupils to new words and expressions as and when appropriate. It is not expected that pupils will learn all the words in the 'Useful words' list in each unit, however. These lists are for guidance only. They indicate the kind of terminology, which might usefully be introduced in each topic, or improve pupils' ability to understand or debate.

Teachers' notes in italics and in panels

The italicised notes interspersed throughout the text are for the teacher's use. They consist of a mixture of hints and tips for classroom use. The notes in shaded panels are lists of potential responses to key questions. The lists of responses are not meant to be exhaustive. They represent a selection of the kind of responses teachers might reasonably expect to elicit from pupils through the key questions for discussion.

Questions

In the final analysis, it is the key questions which provide the basic structure to each unit of work. Although re-wording may be necessary in some cases, it is hoped that teachers will be able to stick fairly closely to the original intention of the questions provided. These questions have been carefully chosen to focus discussion on the issues most central to the topic.

Other things to think about

The activities in the 'Other things to think about' section are purely optional. They are for use when additional time is available, or as alternative suggestions for written assignments and homework. They can also be used to help extend coverage of a topic to a further lesson, if it is thought desirable.

Using the materials

It is not intended that every unit of work should be followed slavishly, word for word. Teachers are free to adapt the materials to meet the needs of their students, or supplement them with material which is of local or topical interest. The book is not meant to be a definitive manual, or the very last word in moral education. Rather it is intended as *a source of practical ideas for the classroom, and a model on which teachers can draw in the development of materials or schemes of work of their own* to supplement teaching and learning in other areas of citizenship, such as law, politics and government.

Experience shows that learning is most successful when it is enquiry-based, emphasising focused discussion work and active learning strategies, rather than a 'didactic' approach. For this reason, teachers should resist the temptation to use the *Good Thinking* materials to preach particular 'moral messages'. The purpose of these materials is not to preach, but *to provide pupils with opportunities for high-quality, meaningful analysis and discussion.*

The role of story

Story has a central place in this book. This is because story is often able to convey the complexity of trying to live in a moral way more effectively than the artificial hypothetical dilemmas sometimes used to stimulate moral reflection. Stories are rich in possibilities. They engage people on a variety of levels - emotional as well as intellectual. Through story it is possible to explore aspects of moral experience which may otherwise be ignored, e.g. situations where what we know we should do is in conflict with what we want, or are under pressure to do. Narrative is thus an important vehicle for moral education. Through disembedding the various moral elements embedded in particular situations, young people are able to build up a practical, working knowledge of morality and moral issues, and develop a framework of moral concepts and language with which to understand and reflect on a range of circumstances.

PLANNING A COURSE

As the units in this book have been constructed in a stand-alone style, they may be used in almost any order in any part of the curriculum. However, they are much more likely to be effective when grouped together (possibly supplemented with additional material) in the form of identifiable modules or discrete courses within the PSHE/Citizenship curriculum. For this purpose, the content of the different units of work can be thought of as falling into three groups:

- moral thinking   e.g.   'The bird', 'Extra homework', 'Great expectations';

- argumentation   e.g.   'Uniform matters', 'Don't try to get round me';

- psychological aspects e.g.   'Hortense by herself'.

Different schools will choose to deliver the PSHE/Citizenship curriculum in different ways. Some may wish to appoint a specialist or small team of specialist teachers. Others will prefer to make it the responsibility of the form teacher and pastoral system.

TEACHERS AND MORAL PHILOSOPHY

It is possible to feel overwhelmed by the sheer complexity of ideas and arguments that surround the subject of morality. In principle, however, morality is no more or less complex than any other area of human interest and concern. That it can seem particularly complicated may be explained, partly at least, by the general lack of opportunity for moral study available within the current education system. Of course, it would be foolish to expect this lack to be made up overnight. Therefore it is important that teachers do not feel they have to be experts in moral philosophy to use the materials in this book. The background notes at the beginning of each unit of work provide the basic information required to get started. In addition, it is hoped that teachers will have access to one or more of the basic introductions to moral philosophy listed at the end of these notes.

THE AIMS AND PURPOSES OF MORAL EDUCATION

MORAL EDUCATION AND CITIZENSHIP IN THE NATIONAL CURRICULUM

Citizenship education is now a statutory element in the secondary-school curriculum. In the 1998 Crick report, *Education for citizenship and the teaching of democracy in schools*, citizenship education was conceptualised in terms of three, mutually dependent, strands:

(a) social and moral responsibility;

(b) community involvement;

(c) political literacy.

This distinction is a useful one. It puts morality at the heart of citizenship education. The Crick report went on to identify a number of core moral concepts central to education for citizenship in a democratic society. These include:

- fairness;

- rights;

- responsibilities;

- co-operation;

- freedom;

- equality.

The essential relationship between moral understanding and responsible citizenship is emphasised in the statutory orders for the new national curriculum. The orders require that secondary-school pupils be taught to:

- think about topical moral issues, problems and events;

- express, justify and defend a personal opinion about such issues, problems and events;

- use their imagination to consider other people's experiences and be able to think about, express, explain and critically evaluate views that are not their own;

- contribute to group and exploratory class discussions, and take part in debates.

They also require that pupils be taught about the legal and human rights and responsibilities underpinning society and learn about fairness, social justice, respect for democracy and diversity at school, local, national and global level. Thus moral development is seen as closely linked to effectiveness in public life.

Locating moral education within a framework of education for democratic citizenship has important implications for the way moral issues are dealt with in the classroom. To these, we now turn.

THE HISTORICAL CONTEXT

Moral education in some form has always been a feature of schooling in this country. Throughout the nineteenth century there were two quite distinct traditions of schooling with two distinct kinds of moral curriculum. On the one hand there was the public/grammar school tradition of education for leadership. Leaders of society, at home or in the colonies, were seen as needing a particular kind of character training - in short, training in the virtues of 'Christian gentlemen'. On the other hand there was the elementary school tradition intended for the 'lower orders' who made up the bulk of the labour force. These were to be trained in the

Christian virtues of obedience and respect - especially respect for the property of their betters.[1]

In establishing the principle of free compulsory education for all young people up to the age of sixteen, the 1944 Education Act did much to bring the two traditions together. With the growth in the ideal of comprehensive education in the 1960s and 1970s came the search for forms of moral education more suitable for a common system of schooling. A number of influential ideas emerged during this period. John Wilson[2] argued for a neutral form of moral education based on a description of the characteristics of moral thinking. Lawrence Kohlberg[3] applied cognitive-developmental theory to moral thinking, identifying a sequence of universal and increasingly sophisticated stages which young people pass through in their growing ability to reason about right and wrong. The Schools Council 'Lifeline' Project[4] developed an important child-centred programme of moral education for secondary school pupils based on the notion of 'considerateness'.

In spite of their considerable influence on educational thinking, none of these ideas has as yet proved capable of providing an approach to moral education which is sufficiently comprehensive and practicable to command general acceptance. Teachers are aware that, however important it might be, there is more to morality than considerateness. They are also suspicious, rightly, of the claim that any approach to moral education can be neutral. By and large teachers agree that schools are not and never can be 'value-free' zones. The question is: *whose* values should we teach?

THE IDEA OF 'CIVIC MORALITY' AND A 'PUBLIC DISCOURSE' MODEL OF MORAL EDUCATION

In response to the question - whose values should we teach? - philosophers such as Patricia White[5], Terence McLaughlin[6] and Graham Haydon[7] have turned recently to the idea of 'civic morality'. There are many different communities in society, e.g., the family, religious organisations, etc., and so on - each with its own set of moral values. But a distinction can be made between 'non-public' communities, membership of which is voluntary, and the larger 'public' or 'civic' community, to which all citizens belong simply by virtue of their common citizenship. The civic community also has its own set of values, which we may call 'civic morality'. The form this takes differs from society to society. The kind of values which ideally characterise a pluralist democracy, such as ours, include: social justice; political equality; respect for difference; human rights; co-operation; civility; respect for the rule of law; and a commitment to negotiation and debate as the proper way to resolve disagreements over public policy.

The concept of civic morality suggests the possibility of a new form of moral education to which all members of society can give assent, but which is also based on positive values. It allows a distinction to be made between the values which may legitimately be taught in schools - indeed, which schools have a duty to teach - and those which are more properly the province of the home, church, and so on (although in practice there is often an overlap). The aim of moral education in schools, according to this view, is quite clear and specific. It is *to equip young people for effective participation in the shared moral life of the civic community* - no more and no less. This kind of approach to moral education has been called a 'public discourse' model.[8] It is the model of moral education implied in the statutory orders for citizenship education in the national curriculum, and it underpins the teaching materials in this book.

A 'PUBLIC DISCOURSE' MODEL AND THE 'BIG ISSUES' APPROACH

What does a public discourse model of moral education involve? Clearly, there is more to moral life in a participatory democracy than simply having a good attitude. Effective citizenship comprises a broad range of moral knowledge, skills and understanding. It involves, among other things:

- a familiarity with moral ideas, language and forms of argument;

- an ability to understand life in the civic community from a moral point of view;

- an awareness of the diversity of moral beliefs and forms of moral authority in society as a whole;

- a rational and consistent set of personal values, and the confidence to apply these in practice;

- a capacity to engage effectively in dialogue with others on issues of shared moral concern.

This departs in a number of significant ways from the kind of approach to moral education often used in schools, which might best be termed a 'big issues' model. 'Big issues' are those familiar and perennially contested moral problems which divide citizens along fairly clear and well-known lines, e.g., religious/secular, conservative/progressive, etc. Common examples are abortion, euthanasia and capital punishment. In the 'big issues' approach pupils are presented with relevant facts (and often representative arguments) relating to a controversial topic, and enjoined to discuss. A successful discussion is assessed in terms of the liveliness of exchanges, pupil involvement, opinions well supported by evidence and/or argument, respect for views which are different, and adherence to the conventions of debate - such as taking turns.

A major weakness of this approach is that selection of course content is largely arbitrary, determined by circumstance or the current news agenda rather than the nature of morality or the requirements of moral debate. This makes comprehensive coverage difficult, and planning for progression and continuity virtually impossible. It is not clear, for example, on what principles one might develop a spiral curriculum appropriate for different key stages. This state of affairs would not normally be permitted in other areas of the curriculum. Typically, one would expect it to work the other way round, i.e., teachers identifying what pupils should learn, then finding appropriate ways of teaching it.

Another weakness is the dominance of an adversarial approach to debate. It means that moral questions which are not susceptible to adversarial methodology tend to be overlooked, e.g., how is morality different from personal taste? what is good character? where do rights come from? etc. At the same time forms of discussion which aid the emergence of agreement, understanding or consensus - all of which are equally fundamental to participatory democracy - are under-valued and marginalised.

Arguably, the biggest weakness of the 'big issues' approach, however, is its assumption that pupils are already knowledgeable about the process of moral argumentation. Classroom discussion is seen as the exercise, not the *means of acquiring* the capacity to participate in serious moral debate. Little or no emphasis is placed on the learning of moral language, concepts and forms of argument, or the development of the social and communication skills which underpin good quality discussion.

In contrast, a public discourse model, which derives its justification from the need to equip citizens for participation in the moral life of a democracy not only emphasises the importance of inducting pupils into the language of moral thinking and debate, it also provides clear principles for selecting and ordering the kind of lesson content through which this can be achieved. In a public discourse model, topics for study are chosen according to the nature of public moral discourse itself. Coverage is systematic rather than arbitrary, and progression and continuity can be achieved through the sequencing of moral ideas and arguments in a spiral curriculum. A range of discussion methodologies is possible, and pupils can be encouraged to identify the types of rhetorical devices and argumentative techniques appropriate to each.

THREE BROAD AREAS OF LEARNING

In a public discourse approach, moral education can be thought of in terms of three broad areas of learning:

1 Understanding moral situations

The ability to understand human situations in moral terms is of prime importance in children's moral development. It is sometimes known as 'moral perception'. It involves a number of distinct capacities, including:

- empathy with the thoughts and feelings of others;

- recognition of the different interests affected in a situation;

- calculation of the likely consequences of different forms of action;

- application of relevant moral values, e.g. virtues and vices, principles, rules, ideals.

2 Knowledge of moral ideas and arguments

The ability to understand and debate situations from a moral point of view depends on knowledge and proficiency in the use of the vocabulary and grammar of moral language. This includes:

- moral concepts   e.g. justice, duty, rights, equality, authority;

- forms of moral argument   e.g. the lesser of evils; ends justifying means;

3 Skills of discussion and debate

To engage effectively in dialogue with others, pupils also need to learn what is involved in reasoned argument, its aims and purposes. These include:

- bringing forward reasons in support of opinions;

- being prepared to revise opinions in the light of criticism;

- listening to and analysing the views of others in terms of evidence and argument;

- defending a case in the face of opposition;

- accommodating difference and negotiating consensus.

MORAL REASONING DEVELOPMENT

Alongside the three broad areas of learning, teachers also have a concern with pupils' underlying level of moral reasoning. As a result of research over the last thirty years we now know that *young people gradually become aware of an ever widening social context in which to construct their moral world*[9]. In early childhood, moral reasoning is essentially egocentric. Judgements about right and wrong tend to be calculated in physical or concrete terms, and authority is seen as external. Children are likely to say something is right because you are told to do it, or you get a treat if you do - or wrong because you will get smacked or punished for it, or the person you have done it to will never be your friend again. A little later there emerges a kind of 'tit for tat' morality. At this stage, children will say it is right to 'get even' with someone who does something bad to you, or helping a friend is important because they 'might do you a favour some day'.

The upper primary and lower secondary years see the development of a more mature level of moral reasoning. Children become progressively less egocentric in their moral thinking. They have a better grasp of the thoughts and feelings of those around them, and are more able to calculate judgements about right and wrong in terms of the effects that actions have on other people. At first, this happens simply on the inter-personal level. They are likely to say, for example, that stealing is wrong because 'how would you feel if someone stole something from you?', or keeping a promise is important because it 'shows you can be trusted or depended on'. It is not normally until later adolescence that moral reasoning takes on a societal perspective. Young people are able to grasp the idea of social institutions as existing in their own right, with purposes of their own, and to which citizens owe loyalty. Only at this stage are judgements about right and wrong made in terms of the needs of society as a whole, or of one or other of its institutions. They may say, for example, that it is important to obey the law 'for the sake of the common good', or because 'the law is the backbone of our society'.

With experience it becomes easier to recognize the different levels of moral reasoning in the classroom situation. The reasons pupils bring forward for their opinions or actions can be located somewhere on a line between egocentrism and abstract, social thinking. Consider, for example, the reasons why it is important to tell the truth:

1	**Self**	e.g. '(otherwise) you will be punished';
2	**Others**	e.g. 'it is upsetting to the other person when you tell a lie';
3	**Society**	e.g. 'truth is essential to social stability and survival'.

There is now a considerable body of research to show that progress towards more sophisticated moral judgements can be encouraged by engaging pupils *in the kind of reflective activities and discussion work which will challenge them to consider these ever-widening social contexts for their actions.*

There are a number of strategies which can be used for this purpose. These include:

- Taking different roles,
  e.g. 'imagine you were x ... what sort of reasons might you give ...?'

- Considering a range of reasons,
  e.g. 'think of some reasons why someone might think it is wrong to ... how many different ones can you think of?'

- Studying conflicts,
  e.g. 'develop a dialogue in which two people disagree about whether it is wrong to ...'

- Reflecting on current thinking,
  e.g. 'why do you think that ... ?'

- Looking to the broader moral perspective,
  e.g. 'what would society be like if everybody ... ?'

One of the underlying aims of moral education, therefore, is the achievement of more sophisticated levels of moral reasoning, for a moral judgement which draws on a wider sphere of considerations will, all other things being equal, be 'better' (in the sense of more adequate or complex) than one made with more selfish considerations in mind. Pupils' moral reasoning development is not something about which it easy to make judgements under normal classroom conditions. This is not to say it is unimportant. It is certainly an aspect of learning that teachers should bear in mind in their choice of learning activities and day-to-day interactions with their pupils.

THE CLASSROOM AS A MORAL COMMUNITY

The idea of a public discourse model of moral education has important consequences for the way we conceive the moral life of the classroom. In particular, it allows us to see the classroom as *a type of public or civic forum*. Each group of pupils is a society in miniature, a collection of individuals with different beliefs and home backgrounds brought together for a common purpose. For most children, the classroom will be the first type of public forum they experience. It is within its confines that they first become aware in a practical way of the spectrum of moral opinion that runs through society as a whole, and that they are able to debate moral issues as citizens. With a few exceptions - not being allowed to vote or make certain personal choices independently - pupils enjoy the same citizenship status as adults. The classroom is thus at one and the same time *an actual as well as a model forum of public debate*. It should be seen as an opportunity for genuine discussion in its own right, not just a source of learning abqut discussion technique or preparation for the future status of full citizenship.

THE ROLE OF THE TEACHER

In the public discourse approach to moral education teachers are both *models* and *facilitators* of moral argument. As models, teachers should try to reinforce through their own behaviour the kind of learning strategies it is intended the pupils should acquire, e.g., by giving good reasons for what they say or do and expecting good reasons to be given by others, evaluating evidence for bias and considering alternative interpretations and viewpoints, and so on. Research shows that where a teacher uses thoughtful, reflective reasoning children are likely to respond in kind.[10] As facilitators, teachers should be prepared to support pupils in sharing their experiences and opinions, encourage them to reflect on their thinking, make explicit key learning points, ensure ground rules are set and enforced, and do their best to create a classroom climate based on respect and mutual support.

INDOCTRINATION AND BIAS

Although there is general agreement that schools are not and should not be 'value-free' zones, teachers may nevertheless be anxious about the potential for accusations of indoctrination or bias in explicit moral teaching. We have already pointed out that in a democracy there are certain values that teachers are not simply free, but are mandated by society, to teach. With issues which divide society, however, it may seem more difficult to know how or even whether to proceed in the classroom. Clearly, it is wrong for teachers to set out to persuade a class to their own point of view. But this is no good reason for shying away from the teaching of issues which are controversial. In a democratic society it is every pupil's right to understand the issues that divide that society, and learn how to make sense of and live with them.

What is crucial is that pupils *are not presented with only one side of a controversial issue.* The most effective way of doing this is to adopt teaching strategies which place as a priority the objective of equipping pupils with an understanding and an ability to recognize bias. This is a long term strategy. In the shorter term, two general approaches are recommended:

- the 'neutral chair' approach;

- the 'balanced' approach.

The neutral chair approach requires the teacher not to express any personal views or allegiances whatsoever, but act only as a facilitator of discussion. There is a danger, however, that if used in isolation this approach may lead pupils to hear only what they wish to hear, thereby reinforcing their prejudices. To counteract this, teachers are advised that from time to time they should adopt the balanced approach, presenting pupils as persuasively as possible with alternatives to the views expressed by the class. One way to do this is to play 'devil's advocate', although care should be taken not to over-use this strategy, particularly bearing in mind the dangers of unnecessarily polarising debates. Summarising and de-briefing is also important, not just in terms of developing pupils' ability to debate, but also in relation to the coverage of issues and arguments.

Perhaps the most difficult thing for teachers to decide is when, if ever, they are entitled to express their own views on controversial issues. As a rule, it is probably best to refrain from expressing personal opinion altogether, apart from when specifically asked to do so by a class.

WHAT IS MORALITY?

THE NATURE OF MORALITY

Morality is a particular area of human interest and concern. Like any other area of human interest and concern - such as art, science, or history - morality has its own language, e.g., 'right', 'wrong', 'good', 'bad', 'ought', 'duty', 'obligation', 'rights', 'fairness', 'blame', 'responsibility', and so on. It also has its own rules and procedures. Moral claims are more than expressions of personal preference, or self- or group-interest. Firstly, they have *general* application. If I believe something is morally wrong, I mean that it is wrong not just for me or my group but for anyone or any group in my situation. Secondly, they are made on the basis of *defensibility*. We make moral claims on the assumption that there are good reasons for making them, even though we may be unable to articulate precisely what the reasons are. Moral claims may never be proved or disproved, but they are subject to argument - that is to say, capable of acceptance or rejection, in principle at least, on the basis of reasons grounded in some common perspective.

TERMINOLOGY

The word 'moral' can be used in all sorts of ways. An important distinction to remember is the one between:

> (a) 'moral' used to refer to good behaviour - as contrasted with 'immoral';
>
> (b) 'moral' used to mark out a particular area of human interest and concern - as contrasted with 'non-moral'.

Failing to differentiate between these two meanings of the word can lead to confusion. In this book, for example, it is important to be aware that when the word 'moral' is used in connection with schooling it does not mean making pupils moral, in the sense of getting them to be well-behaved or law-abiding, but *educating* them in morality, i.e., helping them gain a better understanding of the moral dimension to human life.

The word 'ethical' is sometimes also used to describe this area. In a technical sense it refers to the academic study of morality, otherwise known as 'moral philosophy'. More commonly, it is used as just another word for moral. It is the more common usage which has been adopted in this book.

MORAL JUDGEMENTS

The moral judgements we make in everyday life are of two main kinds:

> (a) judgements about actions;
>
> (b) judgements about people.

Moral judgements about actions typically employ the terms 'right' and 'wrong'. This sort of judgement is most clearly seen in situations where you have to choose between different courses of action. Alternatively, it may be that someone comes to you to ask for moral advice about a choice they have to make. Doing the right thing is not always a matter of positive good, of course. Sometimes it is a matter of choosing the lesser of evils.

Moral judgements about people employ terms such as 'good' and 'bad'. Those which relate to character use the language of virtues (and vices), e.g, 'integrity', 'courage'. Whereas those which relate to behaviour tend to be made in terms of the mental processes, such as 'intentions', 'motives', and 'willpower'.

Not all social judgements are moral, however. Many are rooted in convention and traditional practice. Drawing the line between moral judgement and social convention is not always easy, e.g. in the case of 'good manners'.

VALUES

Values are *beliefs* about what is good or bad, right or wrong, important or unimportant in life. They are the basic building-blocks of morality. The values a person holds help to determine the kind of moral judgements that person makes. Values are expressed in a variety of different ways, including:

• virtues	=	qualities of character, e.g. honesty;
• principles	=	broad considerations to take into account but which do not tell us exactly what to do, e.g. respect for persons;
• rules	=	general prescriptions leaving relatively little room for interpretation, e.g. never break a promise;
• ideals	=	general qualities, or states of affairs, to aim at, e.g. justice.

MORAL THEORIES

Moral problems can be approached from a variety of standpoints, some of which have been developed into moral theories. Moral theories are imperatives which are so general that they are capable of application, in principle at least, in any circumstances. Few people in practice adhere wholeheartedly to a single moral theory. Most people tend to select from a range of them as and when they think appropriate. Common moral theories include:

(a) **utilitarianism**	=	the belief that an act is morally right if, and only if, it leads to the greatest good for the greatest number;
(b) **ethical egoism**	=	the belief that an act is morally right for a given person if, and only if, it brings about the greatest good for that very person;
(c) **Kantian ethics**	=	the belief that an act is morally right if, and only if, it is done out of a sense of duty.

META-ETHICAL QUESTIONS

Finally, there are questions which go to the very root of morality itself. These are sometimes called 'meta-ethical' questions. They include:

- How do moral judgements differ from judgements of personal taste?

- Where do values come from?

- Is human nature intrinsically good or bad?

- What is the relationship between morality and religion?

Needless to say, there is as much disagreement over the answers to meta-ethical questions as there is over practical moral decisions in everyday life. Abstract meta-ethical issues can sometimes seem far removed from day-to-day life, yet the way we respond to them can have important implications for practical decision-making. Solutions to the problem of anti-social or offending behaviour, for example, are almost certain to be coloured by our underlying assumptions about human nature, e.g., whether offenders are capable of reform.

STRATEGIES FOR TEACHING AND LEARNING

GROUND RULES

Successful discussion work depends on the acceptance of ground rules, e.g., not making fun of others, not speaking when someone else is speaking, etc. What is most important is that pupils:

- are aware of what the rules are;

- understand why they are there;

- know they will be enforced.

Some teachers like to establish the ground rules at the beginning of a course. In many cases they will invite the pupils to negotiate the rules for themselves.

There will be times, however, when creating the kind of classroom atmosphere in which all pupils can take part knowing their contributions are valued by others may seem an uphill struggle. The secret is to begin in small ways, setting pupils simple achievable goals (see below) and gradually extending these as they become more able to take collective responsibility for their learning behaviour. Initially this may mean teaching in a very directive way, and giving pupils more freedom as they learn to cope with it.

SEATING ARRANGEMENTS

Appropriate seating arrangements can go a long way towards creating a classroom climate which is supportive of quality discussion work. It is helpful to have two or three different arrangements, conducive to a variety of types of discussion work - whole class, pairs, small groups - which pupils can move between with relative ease. Time spent familiarising pupils with these and how to move between them is rarely wasted. Wherever possible pupils should be able to face the people with whom they are talking. A horseshoe formation - either single or double - is particularly effective for this. It has the added advantage of including space for the teacher. Whatever the seating arrangements, however, it is important to remember that adolescent pupils will often feel vulnerable if they do not have a desk or table to 'hide' behind during discussion.

TEACHING STRATEGIES

The quality of moral debate and argument in the classroom can be improved through the judicious use of a number of general teaching strategies. Useful suggestions include:

- Allowing time for quiet reflection as well as interactive work, e.g. 5 minutes' "thinking-time" in which individuals write down their own thoughts prior to sharing with others.

- Planning activities in which all pupils can be involved, e.g. voting, allocating specific roles to different members of small groups, etc.

- Encouraging dialogue between pupils, not just teacher-dominated talk, e.g. problem-solving in pairs, groups, etc.

- Creating opportunities for pupils to listen to and analyse other pupils' arguments, e.g. paired or small group presentations to the class as a whole.

- Ensuring pupils always have access to a range of moral perspectives on issues, e.g. "What other arguments might be used to support ... ?"

- Creating situations where pupils have to negotiate agreement, or accommodate different viewpoints.

- Where progress is slow, breaking down learning activities into smaller, achievable targets, e.g. "I want two people to explain why they agree and two people to explain why they disagree, then you have 5 minutes to write down whose views you thought were the most believable, and why ... "

ENCOURAGING 'EXPLORATORY' TALK

Research by Neil Mercer[11] suggests that the way children use talk to carry out joint activities falls into three categories:

(a) **Disputational talk** - characterised by disagreement and individualised decision-making, usually in the form of short exchanges consisting of assertions and counter-assertions;

(b) **Cumulative talk** - in which speakers build positively but uncritically on what the other has said, usually in the form of repetitions, confirmations and elaborations;

(c) **Exploratory talk** - when speakers engage critically but constructively with each other's ideas, usually in the form of statements and suggestions offered for joint consideration, leading to new forms of understanding.

Mercer has argued that exploratory talk has particular educational significance. It is a type of language which plays an important part in most distinctive cultural activities in society, e.g. law, politics, and the negotiation of business. It is also an important pre-requisite for effective participation in democratic discussion and debate.

Mercer has shown that the natural incidence in classrooms of talk of an exploratory kind is very low. However, it can be increased through the use of specially-designed teacher-led and peer-group activities. Particularly significant in this respect is *the range and quality of questioning* used by teachers. On the whole, open-ended, exploratory questions are more effective than closed questions which demand a set answer. Questions can be used in a variety of ways to encourage the emergence of exploratory talk. These include:

- Encouraging reasoning,
  e.g. "Why?" "What's your reason for saying that?"

- Developing moral judgement,
  e.g. "Why do you think that is better?"

- Helping clarify points,
  e.g. "What do you mean by...?"

- Generating alternative viewpoints,
  e.g. "Can anyone think of a different idea?"

- Drawing into the discussion,
  e.g. "Who else agrees with ... ?"

- Encouraging consistency of thought,
  e.g. "How can you square that with what you said about ... ?"

- Stimulating a broader moral outlook,
  e.g. "What would society be like if everybody ... ?"

- Helping establish common ground,
  e.g. "What things does everyone agree on?"

- Summarizing the debate,
  e.g. "What arguments were used today?"

ASSESSMENT

Assessment is as important an aspect of moral and citizenship education as it is of any school subject. It is important that pupils are made aware from the very beginning that there are definite things to be learned, and that they know what sort of things these are. This area of the curriculum should not be seen as an 'easy option'. However, as in any other area of the curriculum, there is learning which may be assessed by objective means, and learning which is not assessible in this way.

There are two main ways of gathering evidence of progress in moral understanding and debate:

- teacher assessment;

- pupils' self-assessment.

Written assessment tasks, in the form of one-off moral situations or arguments to analyse and discuss, are useful ways of assessing progress, as are observations of classroom behaviour. Sample tasks will be found at the end of this book. Teacher judgement may be supplemented by pupils' assessment of their confidence at and efficacy in discussion work. Brief open-ended questions at the end of a lesson and self-evaluation checklists can both be useful in this respect.

It is worth remembering that discussion work is a group, not an individual activity. The quality of an individual's performance is closely related to the behaviour of others in the group. For this reason, teachers may also wish to involve students in the assessment of the progress of the class as a whole. One way to do this is to spend five minutes at the end of a lesson summarising the ideas and arguments brought forward, and reflecting on the quality of the discussion which took place.

REFERENCES

1. Lawton, D. (1975) *Class, Culture and the Curriculum*, Routledge & Kegan Paul.

2. Wilson, J., Williams, N. & Sugarman, B. (1967) *Introduction to Moral Education*, Pelican.

3. Kohlberg, L. (1983) *Essays on moral development: Vol II The psychology of moral development*, Harper and Row.

4. McPhail, P., Ungoed-Thomas, J.R. & Chapman, H. (1972) *Moral Education in the secondary school*, Longman.

5. White, P. A. (1996) *Civic Virtues and Public Schooling: Educating Citizens for a Democratic Society*, Teachers College Press.

6. McLaughlin, T. (1992) *Citizenship, Diversity and Education: a philosophical perspective*, Journal of Moral Education, Vol 21, No 3.

7. Haydon, G. (1997) *Teaching About Values: A New Approach*, Cassell.

8. Rowe, D. (1998) 'The Education of Good Citizens: the role of moral education', *Forum*, Vol 40, No 1.

9. Gibbs, J.C., Basinger, K.S. & Fuller, D. (1992) *Moral maturity: Measuring the Development of Sociomoral Reflection*, Lawrence Erlbaum Associates.

10. Wood, D., 'Aspects of teaching and learning' in (eds.) Light, P., Sheldon, S. & Woodhead, M. (1991) *Learning to Think*, Routledge.

11. Mercer, N. (1995) *The Guided Construction of Knowledge: Talk amongst teachers and learners*, Multilingual Matters.

FURTHER READING

Critical Thinking in Young Minds
Victor Quinn
David Fulton Publishers, 1997

Teaching Thinking
Robert Fisher
Cassell, 1998

Teaching About Values: A New Approach
Graham Haydon
Cassell, 1997

Children as Citizens: Education for Participation
(eds.) Cathie Holden and Nick Clough
Jessica Kingsley, 1998

Moral and Civic Education: The Search for a Robust Entitlement Model
Don Rowe
Curriculum, Vol 19:2, 1998

Education for citizenship and the teaching of democracy in schools
Final report of the Advisory Group on Citizenship, September 1998
QCA, 29 Bolton Street, London WIY 7PD

Young people's understanding of society
Adrian Furnham and Barrie Stacey
Routledge, 1991

The Good Child: How to Instil a Sense of Right and Wrong in Your Child
Brenda Houghton
Headline, 1998

Promoting Moral Growth from Piaget to Kohlberg
Joseph Reimer, Dianna G. Paulitto and Richard H. Hersh
2nd. edition, Waveland Press Inc., Prospect Heights, Illinois, 1990

A Companion to Ethics
(ed.) Peter Singer
Blackwell, 1993

An Introduction to Ethics: Five Central Problems of Moral Judgement
Geoffrey Thomas
Duckworth, 1993

Ethics: Inventing Right and Wrong
J L Mackie
Revd. edition, Harmondsworth, 1990

ACKNOWLEDGEMENTS

This book is the result of a curriculum development project run by the Citizenship Foundation on moral education in secondary schools. The project was generously funded by the Esmée Fairbairn Charitable Trust.

The authors are grateful to the members of the project advisory group for their encouragement and support during the development period:

> Anne Barrett, Trevor Finch, Susan Kember, Barry Pinder, John Randall,
> David Rose, Chris Spurgeon, Steve Williams, and the late Victor Quinn.

Grateful thanks are also due to the many other individuals who gave their time to help pilot and evaluate draft materials, or lent their support to the project in different ways, in particular to the teachers and students of the following schools:

> Biddenham Upper School, Bedford; Norton Hill School, Midsomer Norton; Ernest Bevin College, Tooting; Hartshill School, Nuneaton; Beal High School, Ilford; Valentine's High School, Ilford; Ilford County High School; Wanstead High School; Woodford County High School, Woodford Green; Seven Kings High School, Ilford; Middleton Park High School, Leeds; Rodillian School, Wakefield; Crypt School, Gloucester; Hanham High School, Bristol; Barr's Hill School, Coventry; Eastbury Comprehensive School, Barking; Warren Comprehensive School, Barking; Kingshill School, Cirencester; Archway School, Stroud; The Mount School, York; Dunluce School, Co. Antrim; Drumragh College, Co. Tyrone; Ravenswood School, Bromley; Warblington School, Havant; Whitecross School, Lydney; Gravesend Grammar School for Girls; Devizes School; Carr Hill School, Kirkham; St Laurence School, Bradford-on-Avon; Tabor High School, Braintree; St Olave's Grammar School, Orpington; Wolverhampton Grammar School; The Study Centre (PRU), Park Site, Southall; Barking Abbey Comprehensive School; Our Lady of Sion, Brighton; Belmont Comprehensive School, Durham; Henrietta Barnett School, Hampstead; St Dunstan's Community School, Glastonbury; Copthall School, Barnet; Wayland Community High School, Norfolk; Backwell School, Bristol; King Edward Community School, Coalville; Village Community School, Derby; Hardenhuish School, Chippenham; Marlwood School, Bristol.

Special thanks are due to Tracey Ellis and Will Ord of Cockermouth School, and Bill Gent, Senior Adviser, London Borough of Redbridge.

THE CITIZENSHIP FOUNDATION

The Citizenship Foundation is an independent educational charity which has been actively involved since 1989 in developing and disseminating good practice in education for citizenship both in the UK and abroad. It runs a variety of projects, mainly involving young people, to encourage greater awareness of the law, the rights and responsibilities of citizenship and the democratic process. Publications include: *Young Citizen's Passport*, a practical guide to the law for 16-19 year-olds; *Law in Education*, a collection of teaching materials to promote legal understanding in secondary schools; *You, Me, Us!*, a pack of stories and exercises to support moral and social education in primary schools; and *Citizenship for All*, a source-book of ideas for personal and social education with the less academic secondary-school student in mind.

Details of the Foundation's activities, including INSET provision, can be obtained from the Citizenship Foundation, Ferroners House, Shaftesbury Place, off Aldersgate Street, London EC2Y 8AA. Tel 0207 367 0500. E-MAIL: info@citfou.org.uk. WEBSITE: http://www.citfou.org.uk.

ODD ONE OUT
- A QUIZ

AIM

This unit aims to help students to

- become familiar with the idea of morality as a distinct form of thinking

- distinguish between questions of fact and value

- distinguish between questions of morality and personal taste

USEFUL WORDS

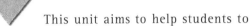

a fact	=	something that is true
a value	=	something you or someone else thinks is of worth
moral	=	to do with right and wrong
ethical	=	moral
taste	=	what you like and don't like
subjective	=	influenced by personal beliefs or feelings
objective	=	factual, not influenced by personal beliefs or feelings
controversial	=	describes something people disagree about

BACKGROUND

At first sight this quiz has the appearance of a normal general knowledge quiz. On closer inspection, however, it becomes clear that some of the questions are not the kind of factual questions which are normally found in a quiz. They are to do with values, rather than facts. Some refer to moral values. Others are questions of personal taste. This provides students with the opportunity to learn how to distinguish questions of fact from questions of value, and how to distinguish questions of morality from questions of purely personal concern.

Notice how young children tend towards moral "realism". To a young child, ideas of right and wrong can be as true as 2 + 2 = 4, or water is wet. In the early years moral judgements derive from unquestioned authority figures, such

© Citizenship Foundation, March 2000

as parents, teachers - or God. Students often need encouragement to see that moral judgements are not true or false in the same way that questions of fact are. Our moral ideas are, in some way, our own property. We agree on some issues, e.g., that torture for fun is wrong, yet disagree on others, e.g., whether it is all right to use animals in medical research.

A common danger children face as they grow older is the trap of thinking that because moral judgements aren't facts, they must be simply a matter of personal preference. When asked what someone ought to do in such-and-such a situation, they may reply, "It's up to them, isn't it?" Students often have to be taught that morality is more than a matter of taste or personal preference. Moral judgements have general application. If I believe something is morally wrong, I mean that it is wrong not just for me or for my group, but for anyone or any group in that situation. Also moral judgements are made on the basis of defensibility. People make moral claims on the assumption that there are good reasons for making them, even though they may not be able to articulate precisely what the reasons are. It is probably true that moral beliefs can never be proved or disproved, but they are subject to argument - that is to say, capable of acceptance or rejection, in principle at least, on the basis of reasons grounded in some common perspective.

THE LESSON

1 • SMALL GROUPS

This is a lesson about questions. One place where you find lots of questions is a quiz. In small groups, try to do the quiz (page 24).

- How many questions can you answer?

- Have you noticed anything unusual about any of the questions? If so, what?

This exercise is most effective when played 'straight' for as long as possible. If students complain that some questions are unanswerable, you can respond by suggesting that the real reason they can't do them is because they are not "clever" enough. You may even wish to offer a prize to the first group to get all the answers right! In some cases, however, prompting may be necessary for students to begin to see that all is not what it seems, e.g., "Have any of you noticed anything unusual ...?"

2 • DEBRIEF

Talk about the quiz with your class. You will probably have noticed that some of the questions are different from the rest. They are not the sort of questions you usually find in a quiz.

© Citizenship Foundation, March 2000

- Which questions do you think are the odd ones out?

- How are they different from the rest?

- What kinds of question are these? Can you put them into groups?

Some of the ways students might group these questions include:

Questions that are up to you? Are about what you think, not anybody else? Have more than one answer? Have no right answer? Everyone's answer is right? Can't agree what the right answer is? Can't prove what the right answer is?

3 • PAIRS

As you will have realized by now, the quiz was a bit of a cheat! The point of the quiz was to show that not all questions are the same. There are different kinds, e.g.,

a. Questions with answers that are TRUE or FALSE

b. Questions about what is RIGHT or WRONG

c. Questions about people's LIKES or DISLIKES

How good are you at recognizing these different kinds of question?

- In pairs, study the questions in **Test yourself** (page *25*) and decide which kind you think each one is. Be careful! They are not all as easy as they might first seem.

4 • CLASS DISCUSSION

Share your ideas with the rest of the class.

- Which do you think is the most important kind of question? Why?

5 • WRITTEN WORK

Think about the subjects at school which have questions of right and wrong in them. Write down some examples. Do you think it is important to have these kinds of question in school? Why or why not?

With younger children you may prefer to work on a display featuring different kinds of questions, or ask students to write up some examples of their own from different categories.

© Citizenship Foundation, March 2000

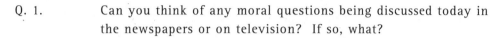

OTHER THINGS TO THINK ABOUT

Q. 1.   Can you think of any moral questions being discussed today in the newspapers or on television? If so, what?

Q. 2.   Some people say that questions of right and wrong do have correct answers, but no one can ever really know for sure what they are. Do you think there could be any truth in this? Why or why not?

AN ALTERNATIVE APPROACH

Victor Quinn* suggests starting by asking students to think of some questions that interest them. They can then talk about their suggestions with someone else, and see if they can decide if they are different kinds of question. The results can be shared with the class as a whole, different types of question identified and written up with examples. Discussion should then turn to the differences between the different kind of question. One way to bring out the differences is to select a few questions and have a go at discussing them in their own right, seeing if different methods of discussing them are appropriate. This sort of approach requires careful direction from the teacher and a clear idea of the types of question one wants the students to end up with. Suggestions such as `hard questions', or `questions with more than one answer`, may need further probing to bring out the appropriate distinctions.  Prompting is also likely to be necessary, e.g., `No one has suggested any questions beginning with "Should ..." yet, or questions to do with right and wrong', etc.

* *Critical Thinking in Young Minds,* Fulton, 1997.

"ANSWERS" TO THE QUIZ (PAGE 24)

1. Paris,   2. Mount Everest,   3. Chess,   4. Eight,   5. MORAL,   6. A pail of water,   7. PERSONAL TASTE,   8. William Shakespeare,   9. PERSONAL TASTE,   10. Deutschmark,   11. MORAL,   12. A (musical) wind instrument, 13. PERSONAL TASTE,   14. Golf,   15. Seven,   16. MORAL,   17. Greece, 18. PERSONAL TASTE,   19. A flower,   20. MORAL.

"ANSWERS" TO TEST YOURSELF (page 25)

1. T/F 2. R/W 3. T/F 4. T/F 5. R/W 6. L/D 7. R/W 8. T/F 9. T/F 10. L/D.

© Citizenship Foundation, March 2000

QUIZ

1. What is the capital of France?

2. Which is the highest mountain in the world?

3. In which game would you find a bishop and a knight?

4. How many legs has a spider?

5. Was Hitler a bad man?

6. What did Jack and Jill run up the hill for?

7. Are you enjoying the quiz so far?

8. Who wrote the play Romeo and Juliet?

9. What do you like to do in your spare time?

10. What is the unit of money in Germany?

11. Is it wrong to test drugs on animals?

12. What is a clarinet?

13. What is your favourite TV programme?

14. In which sport might you have a caddie?

15. How many players are there in a netball team?

16. Is it all right to hide someone's school bag for a joke?

17. If you were having a holiday in Athens, which country would you be in?

18. Which do you prefer? Coca Cola, lemonade or mineral water?

19. What is a geranium?

20. Is it all right to torture students if they do not do their homework?

© Citizenship Foundation, March 2000

·········· TEST YOURSELF ··········

Look at the questions below and put a tick in the column you think they belong to.

	Answer is true/false	Is about right/wrong	Is about likes/dislikes
1. Who made the first computer?			
2. Is it wrong to borrow things without asking?			
3. What do we call a young frog?			
4. Are sweets bad for your teeth?			
5. Should you accept sweets from strangers?			
6. Who is your best friend?			
7. Can a pet be just for Christmas, or is it for life?			
8. 2 + 2 = ?			
9. Why do some people become bullies?			
10. Where is your ideal holiday destination?			

© Citizenship Foundation, March 2000

THE BIRD

A IM

This unit aims to help students to

- recognize moral issues in everyday situations
- become more familiar with the idea of morality as a distinct form of thinking

U SEFUL WORDS

interest = what is good for someone

consequences = the results of an action, or inaction

B ACKGROUND

This is a story about two children who find an injured bird, and can't agree what they should do about it. Matthew says they should put the bird out of its misery then and there, but his sister Sarah thinks they ought to try to find a vet to help it. Before long the debate turns into a full-blown squabble. The story provides students with the opportunity to learn how to see moral issues in ordinary, everyday situations.

The ability to recognize the moral issues in actual situations is sometimes called `moral perception'. It is an essential element in moral understanding and debate.

Notice how young children tend to have a one-dimensional view of moral situations. Lower secondary pupils often see only one side of a situation and fail to recognize the full range of interests concerned, calculate the most likely consequences of their actions or recognize general issues embedded in particular situations. With age and experience children are able to extend the range and depth of their moral perception, and recognize a moral dimension to incidents which they were previously unable to recognize.

© Citizenship Foundation, March 2000

THE LESSON

1 • A STORY

This lesson is about moral issues, and how you can recognize them in ordinary, everyday situations. To find out how to do this, read **The Bird**.

A good way to do this is for the teacher to read the story through first. Then read the story a second time with volunteers taking the different parts.

2 • PAIRS

In pairs talk about the story you have just read.

- Think of some questions about the story. All your questions should begin with the word 'Should...', e.g. 'Should Matthew and Sarah have tried to find a vet?'. How many different 'should questions' can you think of?

3 • CLASS DISCUSSION

Share your ideas with the rest of the class.

- Which of these questions, if any, do you think are about right and wrong?

- How can you tell questions of right and wrong from other sorts of `should question'?

They're to do with: Rules? What you're supposed to do or not do? Situations where someone or something might be harmed or affected? Good and bad? Opinions not facts? etc.

- Are some questions of right and wrong more important than others? If so, which and why?

4 • SMALL GROUPS

In small groups, brainstorm some more 'should questions'.

- Think of some other 'should questions' that arise in family life. How many can you think of? Which of them are questions about right and wrong?

- Share some of your ideas with the rest of the class.

To make reporting back more interesting, you may wish to give each group a

© Citizenship Foundation, March 2000

different topic, e.g., going on holiday, having a party, going to the park, long winter evenings, pets.

5 • WRITTEN WORK

Here are some facts. Make up some 'should questions' about them. Which of your questions are about right and wrong?

a.   Prince Charles is heir to the throne.

b.   The RSPCA finds homes for over 40,000 cats each year.

c.   Children of divorced parents perform less well at school.

d.   Bill Gates is the richest man in the world.

e.   Heart disease is Britain's biggest killer.

f.   Bullying is the biggest cause of truancy among young children.

OTHER THINGS TO THINK ABOUT

Q. 1.   Questions of right and wrong don't always contain the word 'should'. There are many other words which show that a question might be a moral one, e.g., 'right', 'wrong', 'good', 'evil', 'bad', 'responsibility', 'rights', 'fair', 'unfair', 'deserves', etc.
Think of ways of using some of these words to make up moral questions about the story. Can you think of any more words like these?

Q. 2.   How do you think Matthew and Sarah's mum should respond to this situation? Why?

Q. 3.   Can you think of examples of 'should questions' that go with different jobs, e.g. police officer, farmer, soldier, teacher, etc. Which of them are moral questions?

Q. 4.   At what age do you think children begin to ask moral questions? Why? How do you think they learn to do this?

Q. 5.   Why do you think we ask 'should questions'?

© Citizenship Foundation, March 2000

The Bird

Sarah and Matthew stood on the lawn in silence. In front of them lay a tiny bird. Its wings fluttered as it struggled to move.

Sarah was the first to speak.

'Thank goodness it's still alive,' she said.

'Half-dead, more like,' said Matthew, bending forward to pick it up.

'Don't touch it!' shouted Sarah. 'It's not nice.'

Matthew laughed and started to copy Sarah, putting on a childish voice.

'It's not nice,' he said, mockingly.

'If you touch it, the mother bird will smell the human scent on its feathers and reject it,' explained Sarah. 'Let's try to find a vet.'

'It's a bit late for that,' said Matthew. 'The sooner we put it out of its misery the better. I'll get a stone or something.'

© Citizenship Foundation, March 2000

'Don't be so horrible!' screamed Sarah. 'If we get a vet, at least it can be put to sleep painlessly.'

'It'll just suffer more waiting for the vet to come,' said Matthew. 'That's if we can find one.'

Matthew bent over the bird. Its wings were still fluttering.

'It's dying, see?' he said.

'How do you know?' asked Sarah.

'I just know, okay?' insisted Matthew. 'Now, get out of the way.'

Sarah grabbed Matthew as he pushed past her.

'Hey, watch it!' he shouted. 'You're tearing my tee-shirt!'

'I know what I'm talking about as well,' said Sarah. 'You can't push me around just because I'm younger.'

'Can't I?' said Matthew. 'Just watch me. Get out of the way. If you're too scared to kill it, I'll do it myself.'

'No, don't!' shouted Sarah.

She rushed across the lawn and back towards the house.

'We'll see who's scared,' she shouted. 'I'm going to tell Mum what you've been saying.'

Sarah ran indoors, closely followed by Matthew. The tiny bird lay on the lawn, its wings still fluttering.

© Citizenship Foundation, March 2000

YOU CHOOSE

AIMS

This unit aims to help students to

- reflect on what they themselves value most in life

- learn about a number of important human values

USEFUL WORDS

a value	=	something you or someone else thinks is important
an ambition	=	something you want to succeed at
a priority	=	what you put first
material	=	physical, can be seen or touched

BACKGROUND

This lesson features the story of a young boy who has to choose between following a strict training regime in the hope of becoming a swimming champion, or leading the life of a normal schoolboy, having fun with his friends and generally doing what young boys his age do. The story provides the opportunity to introduce students to the language of values, and reflect on the sort of things they themselves value in life. It encourages them to consider not only their own needs and desires, but also to empathise with the needs and desires of others.

So what is ultimately important in life? Over the years, thinkers have tried to identify the essential components of the 'good life'. Many different suggestions have been made, e.g., pleasure, recognition, power, relationships, good health, possessions, inner peace, living in accordance with God's will, etc. Some people have thought that all the good things in life can be reduced to just one: happiness. Others have thought there is a multiplicity of values which sometimes conflict.

© Citizenship Foundation, March 2000

THE LESSON

1 • A STORY

This is a lesson about values, and which are the most important values in life. To help you think about this, read **You choose**.

2 • PAIRS

As you can see, Robbie has a difficult choice to make. He has to decide what he really wants out of life.

- In pairs, improvise - or develop and write down - a conversation in which two people disagree over whether Robbie should keep on with swimming training. You can be anyone in the story you like, except Robbie - e.g., school-friend, swimming coach, mum, teacher.

3 • DEBRIEF

Talk about your improvisation with the class. You can perform - or read - it if you wish. Think about the different choices facing Robbie.

- Together, list the different things you think Robbie stands to gain if:

    A.   He KEEPS ON with swimming training;

    B.   He GIVES UP swimming training.

A.	Fame? Money? A sense of achievement? Honouring his dad's memory? Pleasing his mum? Physical fitness? etc.
B.	Fun? Friends? Freedom? Success at school? A good job? A quiet life? etc.

You may wish to give students a grid on which to record their suggestions:

Keeps on with training	Gives up training

© Citizenship Foundation, March 2000

4 • CLASS DISCUSSION

Talk about the values in your list.

- In general, which of these do you think is the most important in life? Why?

- What other things are important in life? Why?

- What do you think Robbie should do now? Why?

5 • WRITTEN WORK

Do a survey. Ask 5 or 6 different people what they think is the most important thing in life. They will need to give you a serious answer for the survey to be any use. Try to get a mixture of age and sex. Write up the survey and share the findings with your class-mates. What conclusions can you draw from this exercise?

OTHER THINGS TO THINK ABOUT

Q. 1.　　Can you think of other times when people have important choices to make about what they want out of life? Try to draw up a list. Which do you think is the most important? Why?

© Citizenship Foundation, March 2000

Q. 2.   How important do you think it is for people to do well at school? How do you think success at school compares with other important things in life? Why?

Q. 3.   How important do you think it is to please your parent(s)? Why?

Q. 4.   Do you think parents always know what is best for you? Why or why not?

Q. 5.   Certain things we don't like at the time actually turn out to be important for us in the long run, e.g., going to the dentist. Can you think of other things like this?

Q. 6.   Some people think that winning a large sum of money will make their life better. Do you agree? Why or why not?

Q. 7.   What sort of values do you find on TV and in magazines? Do you think they give you a true picture of what is really important in life? Does it matter? Why or why not?

Q. 8.   Do you think there can be times when what one person needs for happiness conflicts with what someone else needs to make them happy? Try to think of some examples. What should be done in situations like this?

An ALTERNATIVE APPROACH

Write down some important values on cards - one value per card, e.g, FAME, HEALTH, RELIGION, POWER, LOVE, MONEY, HAPPINESS, FAMILY, DOING THE RIGHT THING, HELPING OTHERS, etc. Prepare enough sets of cards to go round the class, one set for every 4 or 5 students. Ask students in groups to try to rank the cards in order of importance and think of reasons to justify their decision. Groups talk together about their ideas and see how far they are able to agree.

© Citizenship Foundation, March 2000

YOU CHOOSE

Robbie's mum called him from the kitchen.

'Sit down, Robbie. I've something to say,' she said quietly.

Robbie could tell from the tone of his mum's voice that this was serious. He put down the magazine he was holding, and sat down next to her.

'We can't go on like this, Robbie,' said his mum.

For the last three years, Robbie and his mum have been getting up at five o'clock in the morning, and driving a round trip of thirty-five miles to the local swimming stadium.

Swimming is in Robbie's blood. Robbie's dad was a swimming champion in his own right. He had even competed in the Olympic games. Sadly, he died six months later. It was soon after his dad died that Robbie made up his mind that he wanted to be a swimming champion, too.

At the moment, Robbie is lying eighth in the country in the under-13s. He needs to improve his personal best by several seconds if he is to get near the top. Training takes up most of his spare time. He trains for two hours at a time - once in the morning and once in the evening - six days a week. This puts a strain on his school work. It also puts a strain on his social life. When other boys his age are out having fun, Robbie is off to the swimming stadium with his mum.

Robbie's mum put her arm round her son.

'You know what I'm going to say, don't you?' she said. 'Your coach has been complaining again. He says your mind seems to be wandering in training. You won't improve your times if you don't concentrate, you know.'

© Citizenship Foundation, March 2000

Robbie looked at his mum, and said:

'Yes. I know, Mum. But I've got a lot of things to think about at the moment. For one thing, the teachers at school keep nagging about homework.'

'You always do your homework, don't you?' asked Robbie's mum.

'Course I do,' said Robbie. 'But usually just enough to keep me from getting into trouble. Mr Reiss seems to think I could get into the top set next year if I really tried.'

'There's a simple answer to that isn't there?' replied Robbie's mum. 'Spend a bit more time on your homework, and a little less playing out with your friends.'

'Oh, be fair, Mum,' said Robbie, sharply. 'I hardly see my friends now as it is.'

'Rubbish, Robbie!' said Robbie's mum. 'You were out with them last night when you came back from training, and on Sunday afternoon.'

'Twice in one week!' exclaimed Robbie. 'What's the big deal about that?'

'If you want to get anywhere in life these days, you've got to be dedicated,' replied Robbie's mum. 'Think of all the effort your father had to put in to get where he did. You could be as good as him, if you tried. Maybe better.'

'Mum!' said Robbie, becoming frustrated.

'Think about it,' said Robbie's mum. 'Your name in all the papers. Television appearances. Not to mention all the money that goes with it.'

'I know, Mum,' said Robbie, after a long pause. 'But I'm not sure I want it enough.'

The two of them fell silent. After another long pause, it was Robbie's mum who finally spoke:

'I'll tell you what it is, Robbie. You're just going to have to choose ...'

© Citizenship Foundation, March 2000

THE RING OF GYGES

AIM

The aim of this unit is to help students to

- become familiar with a range of reasons for behaving well

- consider whether getting away with something makes it all right

- reflect on some of the feelings associated with wrongdoing

USEFUL WORDS

temptation = wanting to do something you know to be wrong

conscience = an inner sense of right and wrong

guilt = being in the wrong, or feeling bad because you think you are in the wrong

immoral = wrong

a sin = breaking a religious rule

Golden Rule = a rule that says treat other people the way you would like to be treated yourself OR don't treat other people the way you wouldn't like to be treated yourself

BACKGROUND

This is a story about a man who finds a magic ring which makes the wearer invisible. The ring enables the finder, Gyges (pronounced Guy-jees), to do all the things he has secretly wanted, but previously didn't dare to for fear of being found out. The story, originally told by the philosopher Plato, provides students with the opportunity to reflect on a range of reasons for avoiding wrongdoing. In particular, it asks whether being able to get away with something makes it all right. It also enables them to explore some of the feelings of wrongdoing and begin to explore the idea of conscience.

Notice that young children almost invariably base judgements about right and wrong on self-interest. Avoiding "getting into trouble" is commonly given as

© Citizenship Foundation, March 2000

a reason for behaving well. Fear of punishment or disapproval are, to begin with at least, key determinants in moral thinking. Thus it is common, even in the lower secondary years, for students to think that cheating is all right if they can get away with it. With age and experience most children come to see that the effects of their actions on other people are also important. In due course they may begin to develop the idea of conscience, and a sense of self-respect and personal integrity, and start to evaluate their actions in terms of the effect on society as a whole. But progress in moral thinking is neither automatic nor certain. Children can quite easily get locked into relatively immature forms of moral thought if they do not have the opportunity to experience alternatives.

THE LESSON

1 • A STORY

This is a lesson about reasons for behaving. Does getting away with something make it all right? Or are there other reasons for behaving? To consider this question, read **The ring of Gyges**.

Classical stories have an intrinsic interest for many children. They also enable children to deal with uncomfortable topics at a safe distance. However, there may be a danger that children who are unfamiliar with stories like this might find them too remote from their own experience to be able to engage with them. Where this is the case, you may prefer to re-write the story on a more familiar setting (or, better still, ask an older student to re-write it for you).

There is also the danger that younger children might get carried away with irrelevant detail, e.g., seeing the things he stole floating through the air, etc. Should this happen, direct them back firmly to the main point of the story. You can ask, 'Do you think that is really important to the meaning of the story?'.

2 • BRAINSTORM

Imagine you found a ring like the ring of Gyges.

- What sorts of things do you think you would do with it?
- How do you think it would make you feel?

3 • IN PAIRS

In the box on page 43 you will find a list of things someone might do if they had a ring with these powers.

- In pairs, study the items on the list. Which of them would it be all right to do if you could get away with them? Why?

© Citizenship Foundation, March 2000

- Are there any you should avoid - even if you could get away with them? If so, which? Why should anyone want to avoid doing them?

4 • CLASS DISCUSSION

Talk about your ideas with the rest of the class. Then consider:

- What reasons are there for behaving well - apart from not getting into trouble? How many different ones can you think of?

- Which do you think is the most important? Why?

You may wish to give students a range of reasons to aid discussion. Examples can be found in the box on page 43.

5 • WRITTEN WORK

Here is a list of things which are usually thought to be wrong. Think about each one and write down all the reasons why it might be wrong to do it. Are some reasons better than others? If so, which and why?

     A.   Stealing

     B.   Cruelty to animals

     C.   Spreading rumours

     D.   Not sharing

     E.   Breaking promises

At this point you may wish to re-read the section on moral reasoning development in the Introduction (page 8). According to Kohlbergian theory, reasons for good behaviour can be located on a line between egocentric and social thinking, and between concrete and abstract thinking. The examples in the box on page 43 have been chosen to represent this progression. Note that many of the common religious justifications for good behaviour, e.g., 'because God says this is what you ought to do', cannot be assessed in this way without further evidence of the kind of reasoning that underlies them. To obtain evidence of underlying reasoning you may, for example, wish to ask: 'Why does God say this is what you ought to do?'

OTHER THINGS TO THINK ABOUT

Q. 1.   Would you like to have a ring like this? Why or why not?

Q. 2.   Why do you think Gyges didn't use the ring to help people?

Q. 3.   What do you think the story tells us about human beings?

© Citizenship Foundation, March 2000

Q. 4.   Why do you think the writer decided to 'dress up' up the points he wanted to make in fancy details, such as hollow metal horses and gold rings?

Q. 5.   Why do you think some students risk cheating with their school work when they know they might get found out?

Q. 6.   What sort of temptations do adults have? Do you think they are different from young people's? If so, how?

Q. 7.   There is a saying which goes, 'Be sure your sins will find you out'. This means that even if you are never caught or punished for the wrong things you do, life has a way of paying you back in the long run. Do you think there is any truth in this? Why or why not?

ALTERNATIVE APPROACHES

A.   For a slightly older age group, a different way of engaging with the story of Gyges would be for students in pairs, or small groups, to re-write it in a modern setting with different characters. Ask students what they think the story is about, or to identify the key questions they think it is asking - they can then have a go at discussing some of these questions. This will provide more opportunities for students to pursue their own thinking, but a certain amount of prompting may be necessary to ensure that the central aims of the unit are covered adequately.

B.   This is an improvisation designed to raise many of the same issues.

> One day Tim goes to visit his Aunt Alice in hospital. She is very ill and about to die. When no one else is around, Aunt Alice tells Tim that she has hidden some money at home. No one else knows about it. The money is to be spent on her old dog, Flossie. Tim promises Aunt Alice that he will look after the dog when she has died, and spend all the money on it as she asked. Two months later, Aunt Alice dies. Tim goes with his parents to clear out Aunt Alice's house. When his parents aren't looking, Tim takes the money out of its secret hiding-place. Imagine his surprise when he finds there is over £3000 - far more than will be needed to look after Flossie, even if she lives to be a hundred!

> Tim is in two minds. Half of him thinks he should keep his promise and spend all the money on the dog. The other half thinks there are better things to do with it.

> In pairs, improvise what you think might be going on in Tim's head as he tries to decide what he should do with the money. Each of you should play a different half of Tim.

© Citizenship Foundation, March 2000

THE RING OF GYGES

Long ago there was a shepherd called Gyges who worked for the king of Lydia. One day when Gyges was out feeding his sheep a great storm blew up. During the storm there was an earthquake which tore open the earth, leaving a gaping hole in the ground.

Climbing down into the hole, Gyges saw a hollow metal horse. Inside the horse lay the corpse of a dead body, wearing nothing but a gold ring. So Gyges took the gold ring off the finger of the corpse, put it on his own hand and clambered back out of the hole again.

About a month later, Gyges went with his fellow shepherds to the court of the king to report on the state of their flocks. As Gyges was sitting there, he chanced to turn the stone that was set in the top of the gold ring. No sooner had he done so than he became invisible! The rest of the assembled company began to behave as though he weren't there. Gyges was astonished. He tried it a second time a little while later and it had the same result. Then he made several more trials. It was always the same. Every time he turned the stone inwards he became invisible and when he turned it outwards again he reappeared.

© Citizenship Foundation, March 2000

Gyges could not believe his luck. By making himself invisible he would be able to do all the things that he had secretly wanted but didn't dare to for fear of being found out. He said to himself:

'If no one knows it's me, then no one can say anything. If no one can say anything, then I can't get into trouble for it.'

So Gyges took full advantage of the power of the ring. He did everything he had always wanted. He killed the king. He married the queen. Then when the kingdom was without a ruler, he used the power of the ring to get himself made king. So he was no longer Gyges the poor shepherd, but Gyges the king of Lydia, the ruler of the most powerful kingdom in the world.

Well, wouldn't you do the same?

[*adapted from Plato's Republic*]

© Citizenship Foundation, March 2000

REASONS FOR BEHAVIOUR

Which of these would be all right if you could get away with them?

1. Playing practical jokes.

2. Cheating in exams.

3. Nude sunbathing.

4. Shoplifting.

5. Fare-dodging on public transport.

6. Staying out late at night.

7. Beating people up.

8. Spying on other people.

What reasons are there for behaving well – apart from not getting into trouble?

Here are some suggestions. What do you think of them? Pick out any you think are self-centred reasons. Compare your answers with the rest of the class. Are any hard to decide? If so, why do you think this is?

1. Behaving badly is just wrong.

2. People won't like you if they find out about your bad behaviour.

3. You will feel bad about behaving badly.

4. You wouldn't like anyone to behave badly towards you.

5. Other people could get hurt by your bad behaviour.

6. Behaving badly is not fair on others.

7. The world would be a mess if everyone behaved badly.

8. You will lose your self-respect if you behave badly.

9. Good behaviour is for the good of society as a whole.

© Citizenship Foundation, March 2000

A CHANCE TO TALK

AIM

This unit aims to help students to

- become familiar with the idea of discussion

- reflect on the value of discussion in and out of school

- consider the kind of issues young people have a right to discuss

USEFUL WORDS

to justify	=	give reasons for
to persuade	=	talk someone round to your point of view
to consult	=	ask someone for their opinion
to debate	=	discuss formally

BACKGROUND

This is a story about a class of junior-school children who discover a proposal to extend the length of the school day on two days of the week. The proposal is discovered when one of the pupils, Jayne, opens a letter which she was meant to take home to her parents. Jayne is annoyed that she and the other children have not been consulted on this. Since it is Friday afternoon she asks her teacher if the class can discuss the issue next week. This story provides the opportunity for students to develop a clearer idea of what discussions are, and what they are for. Also raised in the story is the question of the sort of issues that young people should be entitled to discuss - in school and out.

Discussion is a type of conversation in which people consider an issue by putting forward opposing arguments. In the classroom, discussion is more than a medium for academic learning. Learning how to take part in debate, having the self-confidence to defend one's views or argue a case, and the patience to listen to others, are important educational aims in their own right. In other words, learning to discuss is as important as learning *through* discussion. It is an essential element in a democratic education.

© Citizenship Foundation, March 2000

With younger students a good way to begin is by considering some of the different types of talk they are likely to encounter in everyday life themselves, and use their thoughts as a basis for looking at discussion itself, its characteristic features and purposes. If done simply enough, it is a lesson appropriate for any age group from Year 7 upwards.

The lesson

1 • Pairs

This is a lesson about talking. Talking comes naturally to most people. We often do it without thinking.

- In pairs, try to work out all the people you have talked to so far today. Make a list. How many different people can you think of?

- What sort of thing were you talking about? Why? Who started the conversation?

You may wish to give students a grid on which to record their ideas:

Who you talked to	What about	Who started the conversation

2 • Debrief

Share your ideas with the class.

- In general, why do people talk? How many different reasons can you think of?

Pass on information? Ask for information? Fun/enjoyment? Comfort people? Hurt others? Draw attention to yourself? Be sociable? Buy something? etc.

© Citizenship Foundation, March 2000

3 • A STORY

As you can tell, there are many different types of talk, and many different reasons for talking. To find out more, read **A chance to talk**.

A good way to do this is for the teacher to read through the story first. Then read it through a second time with volunteers taking the parts.

4 • SMALL GROUPS

In small groups, talk about the story you have just read.

- Do you think Miss Dawson should allow the class to discuss the plan to change the school day next week? Why or why not?

If you wish to give students some arguments to choose from, a ready-made list is provided on page 50. Ask students to decide which arguments are the best and why. Or ask them to choose one from either column and then decide on an overall winner.

- What sort of things do you think the class might learn from having a discussion like this?

Confidence to stand up for themselves? How to speak in public? What other people think? How good their own ideas are? How to listen to others? Analysis? etc.

5 • WRITTEN WORK

What do you think Jayne should say to the student who says, "We don't need to discuss this"?

- Imagine you are Jayne. Write down what you think you should say.

You may wish to make time, this lesson or next, for students to share their ideas with the class. One way to do this is to ask a volunteer to role-play the sceptical student and think of counter-arguments to Jayne's points. This is not an easy role, and it might be more appropriate if it is taken by the teacher in devil's advocate mode.

OTHER THINGS TO THINK ABOUT

Q. 1.   In which lessons at school is it important to be able to have discussions? Why?

Q. 2.   Do you think there should be rules for the discussions you have in class? If so, what should these rules be? Why?

© Citizenship Foundation, March 2000

Q. 3.   School students sometimes say that discussions are not "proper work". What do you think this means? Do you agree? Why or why not?

Q. 4.   What sort of things do you think schools should consult students about? Why?

Q. 5.   Do you think student councils are a good idea? Why, or why not?

Q. 6.   Are there some things it is better that young people do not discuss at school, e.g., issues that might offend some people? If so, what are they?

Q. 7.   At what age do you think you can start involving children in discussions? Why?

Q. 8.   What sort of things do you discuss with your family at home? Do you feel you are allowed to discuss enough? Why, or why not? What does your family think about this?

An alternative approach

Ask students to imagine what would happen if they woke up one day to find everyone had lost the ability to talk. Use their suggestions as a way in to reflecting on different types of talk, and the reasons why we have them.

© Citizenship Foundation, March 2000

A chance to talk

It was Friday afternoon. Miss Dawson had just given everyone in the class a letter to take home to their parents.

As they waited for the bell, Jayne opened her letter and read it. It was all about a plan to change the times of the school day. The idea was to add half an hour to the school day on Tuesdays and Thursdays. The letter explained the thinking behind the plan, and asked parents what they thought about it.

Jayne felt angry. She could no longer control herself.

'Miss,' said Jayne, loudly. 'They can't make school end half an hour later.'

'That letter was addressed to your parents, Jayne,' replied Miss Dawson. 'You shouldn't have opened it.'

'I suppose not, Miss,' said Jayne. 'But they can't do it just like that. What about my paper round? My village is miles away and I only just get home in time as it is.'

'I expect you'll have to make other arrangements, then,' said Miss Dawson calmly.

© Citizenship Foundation, March 2000

'But what if I can't?' said Jayne, now beginning to sound as well as feel angry. 'And what about children who pick up their younger brothers or sisters from the Infants? Or who've got someone at home who is ill and needs looking after?'

'Junior-school children like you shouldn't be in that position,' replied Miss Dawson, firmly. 'Picking a child up from school and looking after people who are ill are jobs for grown-ups.'

'That's not the point, Miss,' said Jayne.

'So what is the point, then?' asked Miss Dawson, looking puzzled.

'The point is that they can't just change the school day like that,' said Jayne.

'Like what?' asked Miss Dawson.

'Without giving us a chance to talk about it,' said Jayne, insistently.

Jayne thought for a moment, then asked, 'Can we discuss it on Monday, Miss?'

'Surely the time of the school day is a matter for grown-ups to discuss, isn't it, Jayne?' replied Miss Dawson. 'It's not really the sort of thing children need be involved in.'

At this point a voice was heard at the back of the class:

'Let's not waste time discussing ... Let's do something about it!'

Before anyone could say another word, the bell went. The children packed away their things, tidied up the classroom and went home for the weekend.

© Citizenship Foundation, March 2000

WHETHER TO DISCUSS
CHANGING THE SCHOOL DAY

For	Against
It will help students "get things off their chests".	Students have no business discussing adult issues.
It will help them learn how to discuss for the next time there is a problem.	There are more important things to do in school.
Students have a right to discuss things which affect them.	It won't get them better marks.
It will give students confidence to stand up for themselves in the future.	They can discuss it in their own time.
Involving students makes decisions fairer.	They are too young to understand.
It is a way of showing students respect and making them feel involved.	Students don't know how to discuss properly.

© Citizenship Foundation, March 2000

UNIT 6

STOP ARGUING

AIM

This unit aims to help students to

- tell the difference between arguing and quarrelling

- become familiar with some of the qualities of a good argument

USEFUL WORDS

to argue   =   (1) discuss
                      (2) quarrel, or row

an argument   =   (1) reason
                      (2) quarrel, or row

a counter-   =   a reason that challenges another reason
argument

assertive   =   able to stand up for yourself

BACKGROUND

This is an exercise about arguing. Children are often told to stop arguing. Victor Quinn* has suggested that this is good advice, badly worded. What is meant is that they should stop quarrelling. Children need to be taught the difference between arguing and quarrelling, and how to argue well. It is fundamental to the democratic way of life that conflicts of public policy are resolved by reasoned argument, and not by force or violence.

The word 'argument' can be confusing for children. At some point they will probably need to have its different meanings explained. One way to do this is to talk about 'good arguments' and 'bad arguments', and ask students to distinguish between the two.

The exercise in this lesson is based on Neil Mercer's** research on collaborative talk among school children. Mercer has shown that the way in which children discuss develops with age and experience:

© Citizenship Foundation, March 2000

Stage 1:   **Disputational talk** - characterised by disagreement and individualised decision-making, usually in the form of short exchanges consisting of assertions and counter assertions;

Stage 2:   **Cumulative talk** - in which speakers build positively but uncritically on what the other has said, usually in the form of repetitions, confirmations and elaborations;

Stage 3:   **Exploratory talk** - when speakers engage critically but constructively with each other's ideas, usually in the form of statements and suggestions offered for joint consideration, leading to new forms of understanding.

* *Critical Thinking in Young Minds,* Fulton, *1997.*

** *The Guided Construction of Knowledge: Talk amongst teachers and learners,* Multilingual Matters, *1995.*

THE LESSON

1 • BRAINSTORM

This is a lesson about arguing.

- Have you ever been told to stop arguing - at home, in school or somewhere else? Why? What were you arguing about?

Get everyone involved by giving students a few minutes' 'thinking-time' to write down examples of their own before proceeding with the class as whole.

2 • CLASS DISCUSSION

Talk about the sort of things in your list.

- Do you think it is wrong to argue? Why or why not?

3 • SMALL GROUPS

You have probably realized that there are good ways of arguing as well as bad ways. Here is an exercise to help you tell the difference between good and bad arguments.

First, select a topic you think everyone in the class is able to argue about, e.g., where pupils should sit in class, fox-hunting, etc. Choosing a topic from the list you have already prepared is probably best.

© Citizenship Foundation, March 2000

Then divide into small groups, making sure that the total number of groups is divisible by THREE. Each group has to write or improvise a short dialogue on the topic you have chosen. Remember that body-language and gesture is an important part of communication, and something you should consider if you are doing improvisation.

The main task is for each group to be arguing in a different way, i.e.,

GROUP 1:   You are quarrelling. You are talking to each other in a really unfriendly way. At the end of the conversation you all feel worse off than you did at the beginning.

GROUP 2:   You are talking to each other in a friendly way. But at the end of the conversation you all feel you have got nowhere.

GROUP 3:   You are having a really useful discussion. At the end of the conversation you all feel you have made progress.

You may wish to build in an element of surprise into the exercise by giving the groups written rather than spoken instructions as to the way they should be arguing.

4 • DEBRIEF

Share your dialogues with the rest of the class.

- How well do you think each group was arguing?

- What sort of things were the groups saying or doing that helped, or didn't help, the argument?

You may wish to give students some additional questions to help them in the analysis. A checklist of questions can be found in the box on page 54.

5 • WRITTEN WORK

What signs tell you when people are arguing well? Try to draw up a list. Which do you think is the most important? Why?

OTHER THINGS TO THINK ABOUT

Q. 1.   What sort of things can be done to help young people learn how to argue in a more helpful way? Think of some examples. Whose responsiblity is this? Parents'? Teachers'? Someone else's?

© Citizenship Foundation, March 2000

Q. 2.   There are people who are not very good at standing up for themselves even when they know they are right. Why do you think this is? What can be done to help people like this become more assertive in class discussions?

Q. 3.   There are people who seem to like arguing for 'arguing's sake'? Why do you think this is? What can be done to prevent people from doing this in class discussions?

An ALTERNATIVE APPROACH

Victor Quinn suggests dividing the class into small groups, and giving each group a secret note identifying an argumentative "vice", e.g., frequent interrupting; ridiculing an opposing view; making no effort or not responding to invitations; repetitive or overly long point-making; excluding someone, etc. You can match the vices to the class. Each group has to portray their vice in a one-minute improvisation or dialogue. The class tries to guess each vice in turn.

HOW WELL IS THE GROUP ARGUING?

Here are some questions to ask:

1.   Does everyone have a chance to say their bit?

2.   Is everyone being encouraged to join in?

3.   Is anyone making fun of what others say?

4.   Does anyone keep interrupting?

5.   Is everyone making the effort to join in?

6.   Is everyone listening to each other?

© Citizenship Foundation, March 2000

UNIFORM MATTERS

Aim

The aim of this unit is to help students to:

- reflect on the importance of being able to give reasons for their views

- consider what makes a reason a good one

- identify some common forms of moral reasoning

Useful words

persuasive	=	likely to persuade someone
credible	=	believable
tautology	=	repeating the same thing in different words
to contradict	=	say the opposite

Background

This lesson features an imaginary survey on school uniform. Half the responses are in favour of school uniform, half are against. Taken together they illustrate a range of kinds of reasoning, from the use of objective evidence and information to support a point of view, to opinions of personal taste, the barely comprehensible and gut reactions which do not seem to be based on reasoning at all. This provides students with the opportunity to reflect on the importance of giving reasons for their views, and, in particular, consider what makes a reason a good one.

The giving of reasons is fundamental to moral argument. People can hold any opinions they want, without offering reasons to support them. But if they wish others to take their views seriously or persuade them that their opinions are worth having, it is important to provide reasons. Furthermore, if we don't understand why we hold the views we do, we are less likely to be able to stand up for them or feel able to defend them with confidence.

Having the opportunity to explain one's point of view before taking a vote

© Citizenship Foundation, March 2000

often helps to make voting fairer. It confers legitimacy on majority decisions. Minorities are more likely to accept a majority decision if they have previously been given an opportunity to develop and present their side of the argument. It may, on occasions, even allow minorities to persuade majorities round to their point of view. It can clarify disagreements and lead to more mutual respect, even where agreement may not be possible.

Of course, it is not enough just to provide a reason. Our reasons need to be good ones. What makes a reason a good one? Matthew Lipman* suggests that good reasons are ones which are **relevant**, **credible** and help to **explain**. They are also often **factual**.

Notice how young children often fail to give reasons for their views. To them, argument is simply a matter of assertion and counter-assertion. The capacity for rational argument takes time to develop. It is common even in the lower secondary years for students to express themselves in tautologies instead of giving proper reasons for their opinions, e.g., 'I think it's wrong because it is'; or identify with the opinions of peers instead of offering reasons of their own, e.g., 'I think what Mandy thinks'. Students may need regularly reminding of the need to offer good reasons in support of their views, asking: 'Why?', 'What makes you say that?', 'What's your reason for saying that?'.

> * *Ethical Enquiry: Instructional Manual to Accompany LISA*, University Press of America, *1985*.

THE LESSON

1 • A SURVEY

This is a lesson about reasons, and what makes a reason a good one. Everyone knows that you are meant to give reasons for your opinions. But did you know that some reasons are better than others? What do you think makes some reasons good ones, and others poor ones? To help you consider this, look at the survey, **Uniform matters**.

Asking volunteers to read the parts aloud is a way of encouraging students to engage with the topic.

2 • SMALL GROUPS

Think about the things each person has to say about school uniform.

- Try to put what they say into groups:

    (a)   GOOD reasons;

    (b)   Reasons, but NOT GOOD ones;

    (c)   NOT REASONS at all.

© Citizenship Foundation, March 2000

You may wish to give students a grid on which to record their decisions:

Good reasons	Reasons, but not good ones	Not reasons at all

3 • DEBRIEF

Discuss your ideas with the rest of the class.

- In general, what do you think makes a reason a good one? How many different points can you think of?

You agree with it? Most people would agree with it? It tells you how a person has reached a decision? It can be followed up? Or checked in some way? It is easy to understand? Anyone can agree or disagree with it? It helps you to understand how a person has reached their decision? It is likely to persuade people? etc.

4 • PAIRS

There are some reasons you come across time and time again. One of these is what is called the 'slippery-slope' or 'thin-end-of-the-wedge' argument. This is when someone objects to something, not because it is that bad itself, but because they believe it will lead to something much worse, e.g., some people say that legalizing 'soft' drugs is wrong because they believe it would eventually lead to the legalization of 'hard' drugs. There are some more reasons like this in the box on page 61.

- Can you find examples of reasons like these in the statements on school uniform? If so, which and where?

- Where else might you come across reasons like these? Try to draw up a list of everyday situations, e.g., staying out late.

© Citizenship Foundation, March 2000

5 • WRITTEN WORK

Do a survey of your own.

- Choose a controversial subject and ask 5 or 6 different people what they think about it, e.g., whether it is a good thing for parents to choose the sex of their babies.

- Study the answers you get and try to put what they say into groups as before, i.e., good reasons, reasons but not good ones, and not reasons at all.

- Share your findings with the rest of the class. What conclusions do you draw from this survey?

This exercise is likely to be more effective if students all work on the same subject. You can ask for suggestions from the students themselves or choose something topical. Note, however, that what you choose must be capable of eliciting a range of types of reasoning.

OTHER THINGS TO THINK ABOUT

Q. 1.   Do you think it would have been better if Miss Westwood had just taken a vote instead of asking people for their opinions? Why or why not?

Q. 2.   Choose some of the letters from the letters column of popular newspapers. Can you identify the reasons given to support people's opinions? Try to group them as before.

© Citizenship Foundation, March 2000

UNIFORM MATTERS

Miss Westwood is the head of St Crispin's High School. Recently she asked people connected with the school for their opinions about school uniform. Here are some of the things they said.

FOR

'I know it's forcing you to wear things you don't want to. But that's not half as bad as always being shown up by the rich kids in their posh clothes.' (Tiffany, student, aged 11)

'I'm in favour of school uniform because it's good.'   (Todd, student, aged 12)

'If it was good enough when we were young, it's good enough for young people today.' (Mr Pinter, caretaker, aged 52)

'Do away with our beloved garb? A more reprehensible deed one could not contemplate.   Clothes maketh the man, sir!' (Mr Fowler, Head of English, aged 54)

'It makes them look really sweet.' (Miss John, art teacher, aged 39)

'If you let kids wear what they like, they'll think they can do what they like. Then what's going to happen?' (Narendra, student, aged 12)

© Citizenship Foundation, March 2000

AGAINST

'It's just stupid, innit?'   (Niki, student, aged 15)

'Teachers think wearing uniform makes us better behaved - but actually it gets on our nerves so much it makes us worse.'   (Freddy, student, aged 13)

'At this age children are always growing out of their clothes and needing new ones.'   (Mrs Wells, parent, aged 44)

'It's nearly twice as expensive as the clothes they would wear otherwise. Look in the shops if you don't believe me.'   (Mr Delfont, parent, aged 47)

'Teachers don't have to wear uniform, so why should we?'   (Scott, student, aged 14)

'It just looks so awful.'   (Mr Fermat, maths teacher, aged 27)

© Citizenship Foundation, March 2000

COMMON FORMS OF ARGUMENT

There are some reasons you come across time and time again. Here are four of them.

(1)   'Two wrongs don't make a right.'

e.g. just because someone hits you doesn't make it right for you to hit them back.

(2)   'Slippery-slope'

e.g. if I let you stay out a bit later tonight, you will want to stay out later and later in future.

(3)   'Lesser of two evils'

e.g. it's horrible putting the cat put to sleep, but it would be even worse to let it go on suffering.

(4)   'Ends don't justify means'

e.g. it is good to pass your exams, but that doesn't make it right to cheat to get a good result.

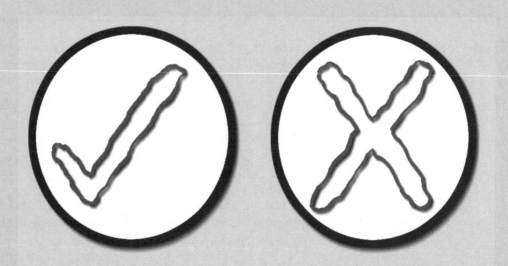

© Citizenship Foundation, March 2000

DON'T TRY TO GET ROUND ME

AIM

This unit aims to help students to

- become familiar with some of the tricks of persuasion

- consider fair and unfair ways of arguing

- reflect on the nature of peer pressure

USEFUL WORDS

a generalisation	=	true in most cases
a fallacy	=	something that might seem true, but isn't
an analogy	=	comparison
a false analogy	=	bad comparison
to dissuade	=	persuade not to do something

BACKGROUND

In this dialogue one character, Ally, tries to persuade Chris to do something that, deep down, Chris knows to be wrong. Ally uses a whole series of argumentative tricks and devices in a bid to get round Chris. The dialogue provides students with the opportunity to reflect on the nature of argument, and consider fair and unfair ways of arguing. Also raised is the issue of peer pressure and what we can do to counter it. Other areas you can explore include the sorts of argument used by politicians, and the nature of commercial advertising and tabloid journalism.

What Ally and Chris are talking about has been deliberately left unclear. So, too, has their sex. By having to fill in the details themselves, students are encouraged to reflect on their own experience of persuasion.

Persuasion is a subtle process. It works on an emotional as well as an intellectual level. There are many different techniques and devices that can be

© Citizenship Foundation, March 2000

used to distract people from the weakness of an argument. By reflecting on examples of these in everyday situations, students can be enabled to become more critical, more analytical and less gullible thinkers.

THE LESSON

1 • A DIALOGUE

This lesson is about persuasion, and some of the tricks people use to try to get round us. To find out more, read **Don't try to get round me**.

One way to do this is to ask volunteers to read it for the class. Students generally find the performances of fellow students more immediate than reading the material for themselves, and are able to engage more easily with it as a result.

2 • PAIRS

In pairs, talk about the dialogue you have just read. Who do you think Ally and Chris are? What do you think they might be talking about?

- Write down two or three possibilities and share them with the rest of the class.

- Which do you think is the most likely? Why?

You may wish to give students a grid on which to record their suggestions:

Who they are	What they are talking about

3 • SMALL GROUPS

As you can see, Ally is trying to persuade Chris to do something which Chris thinks is wrong. In small groups, consider:

- How does Ally try to get round Chris? How many different ways can you find? Draw up a list.

© Citizenship Foundation, March 2000

Twisting the facts	"Everyone does it."
Using faulty logic	"You've broken a promise before (so it's all right now)."
	"Can you prove it?" (if you can't prove it, it can't be right).
	"Remember when your kid brother" (= false analogy).
	"If you can't explain, you can't have much of a reason."
	" ... if you can't tell me how I'm being unfair."
Playing on emotions	"Get real!"
	"Don't be such a wimp!"
	"If you were really my friend ... '

- Do you think it is fair of Ally to try to get round Chris in this way? Why or why not?

4 • DEBRIEF

Discuss your ideas with the rest of the class. People use many different tricks to try to get round us. You can find some examples of these in the box on page 65.

- Which of these tricks does Ally use?

- Think of some other situations where you might find people using tricks of persuasion like these. How many different ones can you think of? Draw up a list.

5 • WRITTEN WORK

Write a dialogue of your own in which someone is trying to persuade someone else to do something that person believes to be wrong - or dissuade someone from doing what they believe to be right. Use as many tricks of persuasion as you can. You might like to highlight and label each one as you use it.

© Citizenship Foundation, March 2000

OTHER THINGS TO THINK ABOUT

Q. 1.   Why do you think people sometimes argue in unfair ways? How many different reasons can you think of?

Q. 2.   Why do you think people often feel they have to do what their friends expect them to do?

Q. 3.   What is the best way to respond to unfair persuasion? Suggest some things you could do or say.

Q. 4.   Has anyone ever tried to get round you in this way? If so, what kind of arguments did they use? How did you respond?

Q. 5.   Do you ever find yourself using persuasive tricks like these? If so, on what occasions?

Q. 6.   Persuading others is an important part of some jobs, e.g., being a politician. How many jobs like this can you think of? What do you think can be done to make sure that people doing these jobs only argue fairly?

TRICKS OF PERSUASION

People use many different tricks to try to get round us. Here are three examples.

Twisting the facts	=	only telling half the story
Using faulty logic	=	incorrect thinking
Playing on emotions	=	making someone feel good, or pleased with themselves

OR

making someone feel bad, guilty or feeble

© Citizenship Foundation, March 2000

Don't try to get round me

Ally:	Get real!
Chris:	I said no way. Okay?
Ally:	Why not?
Chris:	Because I don't want to.
Ally:	Don't be such a wimp!
Chris:	You're wasting your time.
Ally:	Everyone does it.
Chris:	I don't. Anyway, I promised I wouldn't.
Ally:	You've broken a promise before, haven't you?
Chris:	That's not the point. Someone is bound to find out and tell.
Ally:	No, they won't.
Chris:	How do you know they won't?
Ally:	How do you know they will? Can you prove it?
Chris:	Course not.
Ally:	There you are then.
Chris:	Don't be so stupid!
Ally:	I'm not. Trust me.

© Citizenship Foundation, March 2000

Chris: Why should I trust you?

Ally: If you were really my friend, you'd trust me.

Chris: Look, I know what you're trying to do.

Ally: What am I trying to do?

Chris: You're just trying to get me to do something I don't want to do.

Ally: What's so wrong with that? Remember when your kid brother went to the ice rink?

Chris: Yes, so what?

Ally: To begin with he was too scared to go on the ice. It took ages to get him to have a go. But in the end he really enjoyed it.

Chris: That's not the same.

Ally: Why not?

Chris: I can't really explain. It's just not the same.

Ally: If you can't explain, you can't have much of a reason.

Chris: Stop it, Ally.

Ally: Stop what?

Chris: Stop being so unfair.

Ally: Okay, tell me how I'm being so unfair ... because if you can't tell me how I'm being unfair, then I can't be being unfair ...

© Citizenship Foundation, March 2000

THE DEN

AIM

This unit aims to help students to

- explore different ways of making rules

- become familiar with democratic forms of decision-making

USEFUL WORDS

democratic	=	when everyone involved is entitled to an equal say
procedure	=	an established way of doing things
consensus	=	what people agree about
legitimate	=	in accordance with the rules
a majority	=	more than half
authority	=	power
accountable	=	having to justify your actions to someone else

BACKGROUND

This is a story about a gang of friends who build a den on the waste ground behind the houses where they live. Things get complicated when the children begin to squabble over how the den should be used. In the end they decide that what they need are some rules. But how are the rules to be made? The story provides the opportunity for students to explore different ways of making rules. Also raised are questions about rule-making in families, schools, local communities, and in society as a whole.

Democracy is about political equality. It is about everyone being able to have, in principle at least, an equal say in how communal affairs are managed. As the story suggests, what this means in practice is open to question and often the subject of some debate. Some issues you could explore arising from the story include: the difference between the right to consultation as opposed to actual decision-making; the role of discussion and debate; the difference between

© Citizenship Foundation, March 2000

consensus and majority rule; who decides in the end, and how accountable they are.

Notice how the idea of rules and rule-making develops with age and experience. In the early years, children tend to think of rules as givens, put there for them to follow by authority figures, such as parents and teachers. There is little concept that children themselves can be involved in the rule-making process at this stage. Judgements about the quality of a rule tend to be made purely in personal terms, e.g., a pupil might judge a rule about homework to be unfair because 'I don't like homework', or 'You get kept in at break if you forget to do it'. As children enter the late junior and early secondary years they begin to think of rules as human creations made for a purpose - therefore changeable - rather than as givens to be obeyed. Judgements about the quality of rules begin to be made in less egocentric ways. Children begin to recognise that different procedures of rule-making are appropriate in different social circumstances, and that they themselves can have a role in this.

The lesson

1 • A story

This is a lesson about how rules are made, and whether they are made fairly. To help you think about this, read **The den**.

2 • Small groups

In small groups, talk about how you think the rules for the den should be made.

- What do you think is the fairest way of making them? Why? Try to answer the questions on page 71.

3 • Class discussion

Share your ideas with the rest of the class.

- How do you think the way a gang, or a group of friends, makes rules differs from the way rules are made in a youth club? Draw up a list. What do you think is the reason for these differences?

  Role of youth leaders? Accountability to organising body, e.g., council, church? Much larger membership? Not self-selecting? Membership official? etc.

- Which do you think is the most important difference? Why?

© Citizenship Foundation, March 2000

You may wish to give students a grid on which to record their ideas:

Gang	Youth club

4 • IN PAIRS

Think of some other situations where there are rules, e.g., home, school, sports clubs, religious communities, the law.

- In pairs, choose TWO or THREE situations from your list and talk about how the rules which govern them are made.

- Do you think they could be decided more fairly? If so, how? Think of some arguments to support your view and discuss these with the rest of the class.

5 • WRITTEN WORK

One way of making rules is to give everyone a vote and go with the majority. Do you think majority votes are always fair? Consider the following decisions and say whether you think they are best made by majority voting, or in some other way. If majority voting isn't the best way, what do you think is?

    a.   Whether to legalize 'soft' drugs;

    b.   What limit, if any, to put on immigration;

    c.   Whether to restrict families to one car each;

    d.   Whether to make smokers pay for their health care;

    e.   How much MPs should be paid.

© Citizenship Foundation, March 2000

OTHER THINGS TO THINK ABOUT

Q. 1.   Do you think there are times when it is best to leave the rules to other people? Why or why not? Think of some examples.

Q. 2.   Do you think there is any point in being given a chance to talk about rules which you yourself have no power to change - for example, in school? If so, what? Would it just make you feel better? Or would it make the rules fairer in some way? If so, how?

Q. 3.   Can you think of any situations when it might be best for the rules to be made by a single person? If so, which?

Q. 4.   In some situations people elect representatives to make the rules for them - for example, MPs in parliament. What is to stop the wrong people getting elected?

MAKING RULES

1.   Who should be allowed to have a say?

2.   Should everyone be allowed an equal say?

3.   Who should make the final decision?

4.   Should they take a vote?

5.   Does everyone have to agree?

6.   Should the rules be written down?

7.   Can the rules be changed once they have been decided?
     If so, how?

© Citizenship Foundation, March 2000

THE DEN

There was no fixed number of kids in Reuben's gang. Normally it was about 4 or 5. They were all in the same class at the local junior school. From time to time they were joined by 2 other boys who lived nearby, but who went to the school on the other side of town.

During the summer holidays the gang built a den on the waste ground behind the houses where they lived. It was to be their private place that no one else would know about.

© Citizenship Foundation, March 2000

No sooner was the den built, however, than problems began to arise. First of all, Billy told his young sister about the den. Reuben said Billy was wrong to do this because she was a girl and she wasn't in the gang. Billy said he thought it was all right because his sister and her friends had promised to guard the den when the gang wasn't around.

The next thing that happened was that Tom tried to light a fire in a corner of the den. Reuben was frightened of what might happen and thought they might get into trouble. He said Tom was spoiling the den for other people. Tom said he didn't think he was spoiling the den at all. He knew what he was doing and there was no harm in a little fire.

Reuben got really annoyed. Why couldn't other people behave more fairly? He said what the gang needed was some rules.

But how were they going to make them?

© Citizenship Foundation, March 2000

EXTRA HOMEWORK

AIM

This unit aims to help students to

- become familiar with different kinds of fairness

- understand that fairness can mean treating people unequally, as well as equally

USEFUL WORDS

impartial   =   not taking sides

decency   =   respect

entitled   =   having a right to

BACKGROUND

This is a story about Toby who, although he tries his best, never seems to do very well at school. One Friday afternoon his teacher gives the whole class extra homework because some of the kids are messing around. Toby struggles to do the extra work over the weekend, but his friend cheats by copying the work from him on the way to school on Monday morning. When they arrive at school Toby is the one who gets into trouble! This story provides an opportunity for students to explore different forms of fairness, and consider when and how they ought to be applied. Issues raised include fairness at school and what constitutes just punishment.

Fairness means taking proper account of people and their circumstances. It is a complex concept. There is not just one, but several different ideas of fairness: sharing; not having favourites; sticking to the rules; respecting differences; basic respect; making the punishment fit the crime, etc. Fairness sometimes means treating people the same, and sometimes differently. For example, a court of law is expected to show the same impartiality to anyone brought before it, but to recommend different punishments to different people.

Notice how young children often use the term 'unfair' as a label to signify any type of behaviour they don't like, or which they feel is prejudicial towards them

© Citizenship Foundation, March 2000

in some way. Note also how the dominant idea of fairness is of equality, e.g. "If Tom's allowed to stay up till ten, then it's only fair if I can stay up till ten, too." This is why it is often difficult to persuade children that it is not all right to get their own back when someone hurts them. As they become better able to empathize with others' needs and feelings, it becomes easier for them to recognize that inequality can be fair, too.

THE LESSON

1 • SMALL GROUPS

This is a lesson about fairness, and different kinds of fairness.

- Think of some times when you were treated unfairly. What made it unfair? How did you feel at the time?

- Can you see any similarities between different kinds of unfairness? If so, what are they?

- Of the examples you have discussed, which one do you think is the worst unfairness? Why? Try to reach group agreement on this and share your idea with the rest of the class.

To get everyone involved you may wish to give students a few minutes to write down some examples on their own before moving into groups. You may wish to give students a grid on which to record their ideas:

When you were treated unfairly	Why it was unfair	How you felt

2 • A STORY

To find out more about fairness, read **Extra homework**.

Before handing out copies of the story, you may wish to tell students you are giving them 'extra homework'. Wait for the reaction!

© Citizenship Foundation, March 2000

3 • PAIRS

In pairs, talk about the story you have just read.

- What could Toby be referring to when he says, "It's not fair!"? How many different unfairnesses are there in the story? Can you say what makes them unfair?

Being punished for something he hadn't done?

Not being given the usual warning?

Using a different system of punishment from the other teachers?

Not being able to play with his cousins?

Having learning difficulties?

The teacher not liking him as much as the others?

Not getting any chocolates at the end of term?

Toby's friend copying his homework?

Toby's friend not owning up? etc.

- Which unfairness do you think is the worst? Why?

You may wish to give students a grid in which to record their ideas:

Unfairness	What makes it unfair

4 • CLASS DISCUSSION

Share your ideas with the class as a whole.

- Think about all the unfairnesses you found in the story. Can you put them into groups showing different kinds of fairness?

- How do these compare with your own examples from earlier in the lesson?

© Citizenship Foundation, March 2000

- In general, how many different kinds of fairness do you think there are? What are they? (You can check your answer with the list below.)

- Which kind of fairness do you think is the most important? Why?

DIFFERENT KINDS OF FAIRNESS

There are many different kinds of fairness. Here are some common ones to look out for:

1. Sharing equally;

2. Not having favourites;

3. Sticking to the rules;

4. Showing basic respect;

5. Respecting differences;

6. Making the punishment fit the crime.

---

5 • WRITTEN WORK

EITHER   Write a short piece explaining what you think Toby should do now, giving reasons for your answer.

OR   Write a short story of your own. See how many different types of unfairness you can include. You may wish to highlight and label each one as you use it.

OTHER THINGS TO THINK ABOUT

Q. 1.   Do you think it is ever right for a teacher to punish the whole class for what a few people do? Why or why not?

Q. 2.   Do you think that teachers are ever treated unfairly by their students? If so, give some examples.

Q. 3.   How fair do you think your school is? Suggest some changes which you think might make your school a fairer one. (Try not to mention personalities!)

© Citizenship Foundation, March 2000

Q. 4.   Imagine you have to explain what "fairness" is to someone who had lived alone on a desert island all their life. What would you say? What examples could you use to help them understand?

Q. 5.   Why do you think some people treat others so unfairly? What explanations can you think of?

Q. 6.   People sometimes say that life is unfair. Do you agree? Why or why not?

An alternative approach

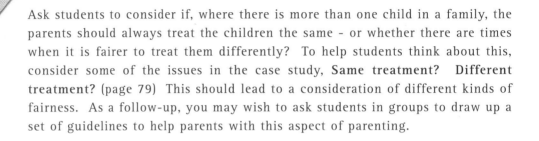

Ask students to consider if, where there is more than one child in a family, the parents should always treat the children the same - or whether there are times when it is fairer to treat them differently? To help students think about this, consider some of the issues in the case study, **Same treatment? Different treatment?** (page 79) This should lead to a consideration of different kinds of fairness. As a follow-up, you may wish to ask students in groups to draw up a set of guidelines to help parents with this aspect of parenting.

© Citizenship Foundation, March 2000

SAME TREATMENT? DIFFERENT TREATMENT?

Mr and Mrs Roehampton have two children: Louisa age 7, and Matt aged 14. Which do you think is the fairest way for Mr and Mrs Roehampton to bring their children up? Always treat both the same? Or sometimes treat them differently?   Think about some of the following issues:

1.   Pocket money.

2.   Staying out at night.

3.   Meal-times.

4.   Homework.

5.   Lifts in the car.

6.   Choosing friends.

7.   Bad language.

8.   The family religion.

© Citizenship Foundation, March 2000

Extra homework

It was Friday afternoon and that weekend it was Toby's birthday. The teacher gave the class extra homework because some of the kids were messing around. She was unable to pinpoint who was causing the trouble, but it was the only way she could think of to stop it. She usually gave her classes a warning before she did something like this, but that afternoon she was too tired to bother. None of the other teachers gave extra homework as a punishment for messing around. They would just give the class a telling-off, or maybe keep someone in at break. Toby wasn't one of the ones who had been messing around, but he decided not to ask the teacher to excuse him from the extra work.

Toby's cousins came to visit that weekend, but he didn't get to see that much of them. While they were playing in the park, Toby was stuck in his room doing the extra homework. What the other students could whiz through in ten minutes took Toby ages. He had always been a slow worker. He found written work especially difficult, even though he had special lessons to help him keep up with the rest of the class. He felt the teacher didn't like him as much as the others because of this. At the end of last term she

© Citizenship Foundation, March 2000

shared out a box of chocolates with the class. Toby didn't get one because he was in his special lesson at the time. Still, he tried his best with the extra homework. He didn't want to get into more trouble.

On his way to school on Monday morning, Toby met a good friend from his class who was in tears. She hadn't done the homework and was scared of what the teacher might say. She begged Toby to let her copy his. He didn't know what to do, but since she was a good friend he gave in and let her copy it.

When they got to school the teacher asked everyone to come up to her desk, one by one, with their homework in front of the whole class. She had heard that some kids had cheated. So she asked anyone who either copied, or let others copy from them, to remain in their seats. By this time Toby was feeling really guilty, so he decided to do the honest thing and stay in his seat. While he was sitting there he saw the girl who copied from him going up to the teacher's desk to hand in the homework she had copied from him.

"That's not fair," thought Toby.

© Citizenship Foundation, March 2000

GREAT EXPECTATIONS

AIM

This unit aims to help students to

- develop the idea of duty

- identify some different sorts of duty

- consider what if anything is to be gained from doing your duty

USEFUL WORDS

a duty	=	something you must do
a responsibility	=	duty
an obligation	=	duty
a professional obligation	=	duty that comes with a job
a legal obligation	=	duty that comes from the law
a moral obligation	=	duty based on what is right
an absolute duty	=	duty you can never be excused

BACKGROUND

This case study involves a twelve-year-old boy called Charlie. Charlie lives with his father and little sister in a flat above their corner shop. Charlie's father is a single parent. He is struggling to keep the family together, and expects a lot of Charlie. How much can a father reasonably expect of a twelve-year-old in these circumstances? The case study provides students with the opportunity to consider what duties are and where they come from. Some of the issues arising from this case study include the obligations family members have to each other, various kinds of professional obligation, and the extent to

© Citizenship Foundation, March 2000

which citizens have a duty to uphold the law and contribute to the future well-being of society as a whole.

A duty is an action which is legally or morally expected. It is something that must be done - regardless of whether we want to or not, or whether we stand to profit from it or not. There are different kinds of duty. Philosophers sometimes distinguish between duties which are determined by roles, e.g., the duties of parenthood, and duties which are determined by some past action or event, e.g., the duty to repay a debt. Some people like to reserve the term obligation for the latter type, but in everyday life we tend to use words like 'duty', 'obligation' and 'responsibility' interchangeably.

THE LESSON

1 • BRAINSTORM

This is a lesson about duty, and the different duties you think people have. To get you started, think about things parents expect their children to help with at home. What sort of things are people in your class expected to help with? Shopping? Looking after a pet? Other things?

- Think of the jobs you do at home. How many different ones can you think of?

- Why do you do them?

> You want to? You are paid to? To keep out of trouble? To please your parents? It's your duty to? Something else?

2 • A CASE STUDY

Are parents always fair in what they expect of their children? To help you think about this, read **Great expectations**.

3 • IN PAIRS

In pairs, talk about the things Charlie is expected to do.

- Is it fair of Charlie's father to expect him to do all these things? Or should it be up to Charlie whether he does them? Why?

© Citizenship Foundation, March 2000

He owes it to his father for all he has done for him? It's the only way of keeping the family together? It's what any child should do for a parent? It's what any decent person should do anyway? It's the law?

Charlie has a right to do what he likes with his own life? He needs to have time to himself? He's not going to have time to concentrate on his school work?

- Which of these responsibilities do you think is the hardest to carry out? Why?

4 • CLASS DISCUSSION

Share your ideas with the rest of the class.

- Of all the things Charlie's father expects, which ones do you think Charlie has a 'duty' to do? Why?

- What do you think makes them duties?

He owes them to his father for all he has done for him? They are part and parcel of family life? They are what one would expect of any human being? They are laid down in the law? They are necessary for a shop to function? etc.

- What, if anything, does Charlie stand to gain from doing his duty?

His father will reward him? His father will like him? It will make him feel good? He would feel bad if he didn't? It will help him because the family will be kept together? He will be a better person for it? Nothing?

5 • WRITTEN WORK

Put the items on the following list into two groups:

A.   Things you think are OPTIONAL,

B.   Things you think are DUTIES.

© Citizenship Foundation, March 2000

Write a short sentence for each item explaining your choice.

    a.   Giving your seat on a bus to an elderly person.

    b.   Paying your debts.

    c.   Helping friends when they are need.

    d.   Having pride in your country.

    e.   Telling the truth.

    f.   Reporting suspicious incidents to the police.

    g.   Having a TV licence.

Other things to think about

Q. 1.   Some people your age never do anything to help at home. Do you think they ought to? Why, or why not?

Q. 2.   What extra duties do people get when they become adults, say at 16? Think of some examples. Which ones do you think are the most important? Which do you think are the hardest?

Q. 3.   Do you think people have duties to themselves, as well as to other people? If so, what sort of duties could they be? Think of some examples.

Q. 4.   What special duties do teachers have? Do you think, say, that if you told a teacher a secret they would have a duty to keep it? Why or why not? What special responsibilities go with other jobs - e.g., being a doctor? Think of some examples.

Q. 5.   Are there any duties that all human beings have - however young or old? If so, what are they? Think of some examples. How can we make sure that people take these duties seriously? Where do you think these duties come from?

An alternative approach

Imagine Charlie refused to do some of the things his father expected him to do. Develop a conversation in which Charlie's father tries to persuade Charlie he has a duty to do them.

© Citizenship Foundation, March 2000

GREAT EXPECTATIONS

Charlie is twelve years old. He lives with his father and his little sister in a flat above their corner shop. His mother left them three years ago. Since then, Charlie's father has struggled to keep the family together. As Charlie is the oldest, his father expects a lot from him. Here is a list of some of the things he expects Charlie to do.

1. Make meals and do the washing up.

2. Take his little sister to school.

3. Keep his bedroom clean and tidy.

4. Baby-sit in the evening when his father is out.

5. Do his homework.

6. Help in the shop on Saturdays.

7. Refuse to sell cigarettes to his school friends.

8. Do well at school.

9. Say "please" and "thank you".

10. Keep his promises.

11. Follow the family religion.

12. Get married and have a family of his own when he is older.

© Citizenship Foundation, March 2000

THE SECRET DIARY OF ANDREA MOULE

AIM

This unit aims to help students to

- develop the idea of rights

- become familiar with different kinds of rights

- reflect on the kind of rights young people are entitled to

USEFUL WORDS

a right	=	something you can claim, or is due to you
an entitlement	=	a right
legal rights	=	rights there are laws about
moral rights	=	rights based on what is right
human rights	=	rights all human beings should have
absolute rights	=	rights that should never be taken away
privileges	=	special rights given only to certain people

BACKGROUND

This excerpt from an imaginary diary charts a day in the life of an average secondary-school student. Reading the diary it soon becomes apparent that the writer, Andrea Moule, has high - some would say unreasonably high - expectations of the people around her. This provides students with the opportunity to reflect on the nature of rights, and the kind of rights it is reasonable and unreasonable to expect. Also raised is the difference between legal and moral rights, the relationship between rights and responsibilities, and the circumstances in which rights may be legitimately taken away from or denied people.

The idea of rights is a central concept in moral thinking. But it can be a confusing one. There are different kinds of rights. Some are purely conventional and have their origins in the law, e.g. the right to vote at 18.

© Citizenship Foundation, March 2000

Others are more general and have their origins in ideas of human nature, e.g. the right to be treated with respect. There are 'claim'-rights - rights we claim from other people, such as the right to an education, and 'liberties' - rights that allow us freedom to pursue our interests unhindered by others, such as the right to free speech. A further confusion is that people often seem to think that by simply saying one has a right, that right is automatically granted to us. But, as the scenario in this unit suggests, no one gets a right simply by ascribing it to themselves. There has to be a good reason for it.

Notice how most young children are already familiar with the term 'rights', even though they probably don't use it much in everyday conversation. One of the aims of this unit is to encourage students to use the term more regularly, but to use it appropriately and with understanding. In the early years, children think of a right as a kind of rule. They will happily talk about having a right to get on with their work. But they tend to see it as just another rule made by the teacher. Later on they conceive rights in terms of needs or preferences, e.g. they think that people have a right to property because they might not like their things stolen. Rooting rights in ideas of human dignity or social harmony takes longer, and often considerable encouragement, to develop.

T**HE LESSON**

1 • A story

This is a lesson about rights, and the kind of rights we are entitled to. To find out more about rights, read **The secret diary of Andrea Moule**.

2 • In pairs

As you can see, Andrea *thinks* she has lots of rights. Look back over things she writes in her diary.

- What rights does Andrea think she has? In pairs, draw up a list. How many different ones can you find?

© Citizenship Foundation, March 2000

The right to:

      have her breakfast made?

      a birthday present?

      be free from bullying?

      property?

      a punctual bus service?

      a seat on the bus?

      smoke on the bus?

      get her money back when thrown off the bus?

      walk in a cycle lane?

      a calculator in Maths?

      play football in PE?

      refuse to go to detention?

      answer back a teacher?

      be provided with food if she has no money?

      tell the supervisor what to do?

      dress how she likes?

      be free from verbal abuse?

      miss guitar lessons if she feels like it?

      a decent education?

      go home from school if she feels like it? etc.

You may wish to give students some suggestions to assist their thinking (see list above). What rights does Andrea have? a. As a child? b. As a passenger? c. As a school student? d. As a girl? e. As a citizen? f. As a human being?

3 • CLASS DISCUSSION

Share what you have found with the rest of the class.

- Do you think it is reasonable of Andrea to think she has all these rights? Or is she expecting too much? What do you think? Why?

- Which of these rights do you think she *really* has? Why?

4 • IN PAIRS

Rights can be grouped in different ways. One way is to decide whether they are legal or moral rights. A legal right is one which there is a law about. A moral right is a one which is based simply on what is right. Think about the rights you decided that Andrea has.

© Citizenship Foundation, March 2000

- In pairs, try to decide whether they are:

    a.   LEGAL rights, or

    b.   MORAL rights.

- Can you think of any other kinds of rights? If so, what?

Human rights? Rights at work? The rights of the child? Consumers' rights? Animal rights? etc.

- Discuss your ideas with the rest of the class.

5 • WRITTEN WORK

An example of a right given by the law is the right to vote in a general election. In recent years the right to vote has come down from 21 to 18. Do you think that the law should now be changed to give this right to children? Write a short piece expressing your views on this. Try to look at reasons for and against the idea before you set down your conclusion.

OTHER THINGS TO THINK ABOUT

Q. 1.   What rights does Andrea have that everyone else in the world should have?

Q. 2.   Andrea had her right to travel on the bus taken away. What other rights were taken away in the story? How were they taken away? Do you think it was right that they were taken away?

Q. 3.   Are there some rights that should never be taken away? If so, which? Why should they never be taken away?

Q. 4.   You can tell from the story that rights are often closely associated with duties. Try to find some examples in the story where they are associated with duties, and some where they are not.

Q. 5.   Andrea isn't the only person in the story with rights. Which other people in the story have rights? What kind of rights are they?

© Citizenship Foundation, March 2000

THE SECRET DIARY OF ANDREA MOULE

Thursday (two days to my birthday!)

8.01 a.m.   Got up. My beloved mother was still refusing to make breakfast. Said my behaviour at the swimming pool last week was the final straw. From now on I've got to make my own breakfast. No time this morning, though. Too much of a rush. Not much chance of a birthday present on Sunday now, I suppose. Something ought to be done about mothers like mine!

8.22 a.m.   Ambushed at the bus stop. (Year 10 boys!) Took some of my dinner money and put soil down the back of my blouse. Who do they think they are?

8.32 a.m.   Bus late as usual. I don't know why they bother to put up timetables. Worse still, the last seat was taken by some grotty old bloke who got on just before me. So I lit up a cigarette and blew

© Citizenship Foundation, March 2000

smoke in his direction. Cool! The old bloke reported me to the bus driver, and I got thrown off. Didn't even get my money back. The cheek!

8.37 a.m.   Nearly run over by a bog-eyed cyclist. Made me drop my school bag in a puddle. He muttered something about "cycle lanes" - whatever they are - and started telling me off. He is the one who should be told off, not me. My school bag is a real mess!

10.15 a.m.   Maths! What a nightmare! Not enough calculators to go round, and I was the one who had to do without. It's not fair! My friend goes to St Chad's School, and they all have a calculator there. (AND girls can play football in PE!) Complained about my lack of calculator to the teacher. He made some feeble excuse, and asked me why I hadn't turned up to his detention yesterday afternoon. I asked him why he hadn't given me a calculator, and he gave me another detention! Honestly! Can't the man take a joke?

12.30 p.m.   Lunch-time. Only enough money to buy a packet of crisps. (Year 10 boys!!) Told the supervisor she should make arrangements for people who have their dinner-money stolen. Got a mouthful of abuse in return. But no extra food. Not even a measly chip!

12.57 p.m.   Head of Year said I looked like a "tart". Told me to tuck in my blouse and smarten myself up. She's got room to talk! Old bag!

1.12 p.m.   Bumped into Mr Bream. Remembered - too late - that I promised him I would turn up for my guitar lesson today. (Forgot last Thursday.) (And the Thursday before!) He was annoyed because he had been sitting waiting in the practice room. Can't see why. What's the man paid for? He should have been pleased I signed up for his mouldy lessons in the first place!

1.17 p.m.   Still starving hungry. Couldn't stand the thought of staying at school all afternoon on an empty stomach. Wouldn't get a decent education if I did. Decided to go home.

1.19 p.m.   Went home.

© Citizenship Foundation, March 2000

A SPLENDID IDEA

Aim

This unit aims to help students to

- reflect on the process of moral decision-making

- consider different sources of moral authority

Word power

self-interest   =   what is good for you yourself

compassion   =   strongly feeling sorry for someone

empathy   =   understanding what another person is thinking or feeling

moral   =   the power to decide what is right and wrong
authority

Background

This pastiche on Kenneth Grahame's *The Wind in the Willows* tells the story of a group of animals who stumble across a baby snake while out walking in the woods. The snake appears to be in need of help - but it is poisonous. What are the animals to do? Leave the snake where it is? Or help it in some way? Each of the creatures approaches the question in a different way. The Mole's instinct is to act out of compassion, regardless of the consequences for himself. He puts himself in the position of the baby snake and imagines how he would feel. His is a very emotional response. In contrast, the Rat consistently puts himself and his own interests first. He only agrees with the rest so as not to appear different. Mr Toad bows to the higher authority of Owl. His is a much more principled response. The Badger is much more trusting of his own judgement. He thinks through the situation carefully and considers the consequences of the different options. Taken together, the different animals represent the human experience of moral decision-making and the internal conflict which often goes with it. The story provides students with the opportunity to examine alternative approaches to decision-making, and the different sources of moral authority which underpin them.

© Citizenship Foundation, March 2000

Some students may find the idea of a children's story a little below them. If you think there are likely to be difficulties with your students, you may prefer an alternative approach, such as the one outlined at the end of these notes.

Notice that, although young students rarely have difficulty expressing a view on moral issues, reflecting on the nature and origin of these views can be much more difficult. The ability to think critically about one's own thinking is still developing in the top junior and lower secondary years, and students may need some encouragement with this kind of exercise.

THE LESSON

1 • A STORY

This is a lesson about moral decisions, and how people make them. To find out more, read A **splendid idea!**

A good way to do this is for the teacher to read the story through first. Then read the story a second time with volunteers taking the different parts.

2 • IN PAIRS

As you can see, the animals in the story have a moral problem to solve. They have to decide whether or not they should try to help the baby adder.

- In pairs, talk about the way the animals dealt with the problem. Can you spot any differences between the animals? If so, what?

> Mole: Acting on feelings rather than reason? Imagining what he would feel like in the snake's position? With kindness and compassion? Not thinking about the consequences for himself? Getting too worked up to think straight?
>
> Rat: Thinking only about himself? Concerned about what the others might think of him?
>
> Badger: Thinking about everyone involved? Acting on reason? Not letting his emotions get the better of him?
>
> Mr Toad: Applying principles? Following a higher moral authority?

- Discuss what you have found with the rest of the class.

© Citizenship Foundation, March 2000

You may wish to give students a grid on which to record their thinking:

Mole	Rat	Badger	Mr Toad

3 • SMALL GROUPS

Human beings are much more complex than animals, of course. We all have a little bit of each of the animals in the story inside us.

- In small groups consider the following problems, and try to imagine how you would respond if you were behaving like the Mole (i.e., with compassion). Then imagine you were like the Rat (i.e., self-centred), Toad (i.e., following a higher moral authority) and Badger (i.e., using a reasoned approach).

  A.   A beggar asks you for money.

  B.   A member of your family asks you to lie to keep them from getting into trouble.

  C.   You see someone being beaten up after school and recognise the bullies - but you also know that they have seen you.

You may wish to give students a grid on which to record their thinking:

	Mole	Rat	Badger	Mr Toad
A				
B				
C				

4 • CLASS DISCUSSION

Discuss your ideas with the rest of the class.

- Do you think any of these forms of moral reasoning are better than others? If so, which and why? You may wish to draw up a list of the plus and minus points of each one before deciding.

© Citizenship Foundation, March 2000

Minus points might include:

Acting on emotion may blind you to other important moral factors. It may also prejudice you against people for whom you have little natural sympathy.

Always putting yourself first is selfishness.

Following a higher authority brings with it the risk that the higher authority may be wrong; that you mistake what the higher authority is saying; or that you choose the wrong authority.

Moral principles can be interpreted in many different ways.

Thinking about consequences doesn't guarantee you a solution, you also have to decide which consequences are the most important ones.

5 • WRITTEN WORK

Imagine you are advising a younger brother or sister - say, someone about 5 or 6 - about what they should do when they have a tricky moral problem to solve. Write a short piece outlining what you would say. One way to do this is to draw up a list of simple do's and don'ts. When you have finished, add a further few lines explaining the thinking behind your choice of advice.

OTHER THINGS TO THINK ABOUT

Q. 1.   Do you, like Mr Toad, think that rather than trust your own judgement, you should follow someone else's? Who do you think is the best to follow? Why?

Q. 2.   People sometimes say their conscience tells them how to behave. What is a conscience? Where does it come from? Do you think it can ever be wrong? Is it different from the forms of moral reasoning you've talked about so far? If so, how?

Q. 3.   The law also tells people how to behave. Do you think it can always be trusted? Why or why not?

Q. 4.   Do you think it is always selfish to put yourself first? Why or why not?

Q. 5.   What do you think Owl stands for? Think of some possibilities. How many different ones can you think of?

© Citizenship Foundation, March 2000

AN ALTERNATIVE APPROACH

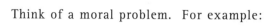

Think of a moral problem. For example:

> A friend who is addicted to gambling on fruit machines asks you for a loan. She says it is just until she gets paid.

Allocate character cards to students in pairs or small groups, as follows:

Mr. Heart   You are the sort of person who is kindhearted, forgiving and trusting. You are always sympathetic towards other people's needs.

Mrs Brain   You are the sort of person who doesn't let your emotions get the better of you. You are always careful. You weigh up the evidence on both sides before making a decision.

Ms Self   You are the sort of person who always puts yourself first. You believe that if you don't look after yourself, no one else will.

Mr Monk   You are a religious person. You try to base all the decisions you make on your religion.

Students have to respond to the problem in the character of the person given to them on the card.

© Citizenship Foundation, March 2000

A splendid idea!

The three animals walked side by side, silently, through the Wild Wood. Each of them was deep in thought. Then, all of a sudden, the Rat stopped dead in its tracks. Its whiskers began to quiver.

'What's that?' asked the Rat, pointing ahead.

The three animals edged forward to get a better look.

'It's an adder,' whispered the Badger.

'What's an adder?' asked the Mole.

'It's a type of snake,' replied the Badger.

'What's wrong with it?' asked the Rat. 'It's not moving.'

'It's only a baby,' said the Badger. 'I think it's lost its parents.'

'What should we do?' asked the Rat nervously, twitching its whiskers.

'We can't leave it here all on its own,' said the Mole, beginning to cry. 'I'd hate to be left all on my own in the Wild Wood. Let's pick it up and take it home with us.'

'Wait,' the Badger shouted. 'Don't you know adders are poisonous?'

'I hadn't thought of that,' said the Rat, looking quite worried. 'Perhaps we'd better leave it where it is. Someone else is bound to find it. Come on, you two. Let's get going.'

'We can't leave it all on its own,' said the Mole, sobbing.

'Maybe not, but you've got to think of yourself as well,' said the Badger, putting a friendly paw round the Mole's velvet shoulder.

'Quite right,' said the Rat, still twitching its whiskers. 'We've got to think of ourselves.'

© Citizenship Foundation, March 2000

Just at that moment, Mr Toad strolled into view.

'What's the matter, everyone?' asked Mr Toad. 'You all look so serious.'

'Nothing's the matter,' said the Rat, sharply.

'Yes, there is!' the Mole said, still trying to fight back the tears. 'There's a little baby adder. It's all on its own. There's no one to look after it.'

'We're not sure what to do,' the Badger said. 'It's probably poisonous.'

'Owl says we must love and respect all woodland creatures,' said Mr Toad, confidently.

'What? Even if they're poisonous?' asked the Rat, annoyed.

'That's what Owl says,' repeated Mr Toad.

'How does Owl know?' asked the Rat, suspiciously.

But before Mr Toad had time to answer, the Badger had an idea.

'I've an idea. Mr Toad's right. Snakes are woodland creatures like us. It wouldn't be right to leave a baby to die. We'd feel terrible if we did. But if it is poisonous, we could be putting our lives at risk. So why don't we pick it up with stick and put it into a sack? We could carry it home in the sack and give it something to eat. Then, tomorrow, we can find out where its parents are. How about it?'

'A splendid idea!' said the Mole and Mr Toad together.

Then the Badger turned to the Rat.

'Well, Rat? What do you think?' asked the Badger.

'Okay,' said the Rat, trying to sound enthusiastic. 'But I want to carry the sack.'

[with apologies to Kenneth Grahame]

© Citizenship Foundation, March 2000

HORTENSE BY HERSELF

AIM

This unit aims to help students to

- understand how someone's self-image can affect their behaviour

- consider the origins of self-image

- reflect on their own self-image

WORD POWER

self-image	=	how you see yourself
ideal self-image	=	how you like to think of yourself
actual self-image	=	how you think you really are
self-esteem	=	how good you feel about yourself
a delusion	=	a false belief
an inferiority complex	–	doing yourself down because you think you are bad at something
a self-fulfilling prophecy	=	being treated as a certain kind of person so often that you eventually begin to behave that way

BACKGROUND

This is a story about a sparrow with an inferiority complex. Hortense is the last of the chicks to be hatched. She is also the smallest. Unable to cope with the teasing and name-calling from her brothers and sisters, Hortense gradually convinces herself that she is not really a sparrow at all - but an eagle. With this in mind she rather pathetically sets out to acquire the characteristics of a bird of prey. The story provides students with the opportunity to consider how a person's image of him/herself can affect their behaviour, and, ultimately, their direction in life. It raises the question of how the sense of self develops, and what if anything can be done to help people develop a positive image of themselves and their achievements. Some of the issues you could explore

© Citizenship Foundation, March 2000

arising from this story include: the effects of bullying, the nature of peer group pressure, and the effects of advertising and the mass media on the way people see themselves.

As we go through life we each build up an image of ourselves, a view of what we are like and how we are seen by others. This image can have a powerful effect on our moral outlook and how we relate to others. Wanting to be liked by others is an important determinant of human behaviour. So, too, is how comfortable we are with the image we have of ourselves. Problems can arise when the person we would like to be seen as is very different from the person we actually think we are. Low self-esteem can be the result of a shortfall between the two.

Notice how the source of a child's ideal self-image tends to change over time. To begin with young children tend to identify with their parents. By the time they reach top junior or lower secondary level, however, they have become much more likely to identify themselves with peers. Ideal self-image at this stage is often a composite of the characteristics thought desirable in, or expected by, friends.

THE LESSON

1 • A STORY

This is a lesson about the way we see ourselves, and how this affects our behaviour. To find out more, read **Hortense by herself**.

2 • IN PAIRS

Talk about the way Hortense starts to change as she grows up.

- What changes do the sparrows begin to notice in Hortense as she gets older? Draw up a list.

> Starts to think she isn't a sparrow. Stops chirruping? Tries silent hovering? Refuses sparrow food? Becomes more confident and able to stand up for herself, and appears more than a little arrogant?

- Share your ideas with the rest of the class. Were there some things you failed to spot?

© Citizenship Foundation, March 2000

3 • SMALL GROUPS

In small groups, talk about the reasons why you think Hortense begins to change.

- What do you think is making Hortense change in this way? How many different reasons can you think of?

> The others are picking on her? It helps protect her from the bullying? She doesn't like being a sparrow? The other sparrows set her an ideal it is impossible to live up to? She thinks it will give her something which the others will look up to? It draws attention away from her weaknesses? It makes her feel better than the others? etc.

- Why do you think she doesn't stop before it is too late?

> The others would make even more fun of her? It would mean admitting she was a failure? She has really convinced herself she is an eagle? She doesn't realize the danger which awaits her? etc.

- Whose fault do you think it was that she died? Her own, or her family's? Why?

> Her own fault?
>
> > She should have paid no attention to the name-calling? She knew she wasn't really an eagle? She should have been satisfied with who she was? It was her choice? She should have stopped before it was too late? etc.
>
> Her family's fault?
>
> > Calling her names? Bullying her? Making her feel bad about herself? Didn't give her the extra attention she needed? etc.

4 • CLASS DISCUSSION

Discuss your ideas with the rest of the class.

- Think of other examples of the way a person's image of themselves can affect their behaviour. How many different ones can you think of?

  Students who like to think they are 'hard', or fear they are seen as a 'swot', etc.?

© Citizenship Foundation, March 2000

• Do you think there are advantages and disadvantages to having a certain kind of self-image? If so, what?

5 • WRITTEN WORK

Schools can sometimes make students feel they are failures. Think of some ways in which this can happen. How does it make people behave? Write a short piece about this, saying what you think schools should do about this.

OR

Re-write the story of Hortense putting it in an everyday setting with human characters.

OTHER THINGS TO THINK ABOUT

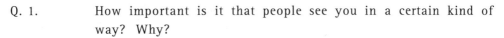

Q. 1.   How important is it that people see you in a certain kind of way? Why?

Q. 2.   The young sparrows were very cruel to Hortense. Why do you think young children are often so unkind to others? At what age do you think they grow out of this kind of behaviour?

Q. 3.   These days it is thought to be all right for boys to be seen as more caring and girls as more ambitious or competitive than they used to be seen. What do you think are the advantages and disadvantages of this?

Q. 4.   What sorts of thing can parents do to help their children grow up feeling positive about themselves? Draw up a list. Which do you think is the most important? Why?

Q. 5.   Do you think it is selfish to like yourself? Why or why not?

Q. 6.   How do advertisers try to play on the way we like to see ourselves? Collect some examples of adverts from TV or magazines. Do you think what they do is fair? Why or why not?

© Citizenship Foundation, March 2000

Hortense by herself

Hortense was the last of the chicks to be hatched. She was also the smallest. Her feathers were slow to develop, and she was the last to learn how to fly.

Hortense was picked on because she was different. Young sparrows can be very cruel. She couldn't keep up with her brothers and sisters in the air when they challenged her to races. Hortense could not decide which was worse: being called names for not accepting the challenge, or being called names for accepting the challenge and losing.

When she was a few months old, Hortense's family began to notice something odd about her. She got the idea - nobody knows where from - that she was not really a sparrow at all. She stopped making the chirruping sound that sparrows usually make. Instead, she began hovering silently in the air - or trying her best to. (Hovering silently is a very difficult thing for a sparrow to do.) She refused to eat the food that all the other sparrows ate. She said she preferred baby voles and fieldmice.

Hortense's family did not know what to make of it all. She told them there must have been some mistake when she was hatched. She said she was really a bird of prey, a golden eagle or something like that.

Still the other birds teased her. But the teasing didn't seem to hurt as much as it did before. Hortense seemed much more confident and able to stand up for herself. Should one of the other sparrows try to make fun of her pathetic attempts to soar or swoop, she said they just did not understand. She told them it took a long time to learn to be a golden eagle. There was much more to it than

© Citizenship Foundation, March 2000

being a sparrow. There were times when they thought Hortense had become far too big for her boots!

As time went on, Hortense became more and more certain she was a golden eagle. The fact that she still looked like a sparrow seemed to make no difference. The pretence was fooling no one. No one, that is, except Hortense herself.

When spring came, Hortense announced she was leaving for Scotland. Eagles usually make their nests on high, rocky ledges. There were no high, rocky ledges where Hortense lived. So she said goodbye to her family and flew north.

A few days later, Hortense arrived on a Scottish mountainside. It was then that she found herself, for the first time in her life, face to face with a real golden eagle ... which promptly tore her to pieces and fed her to its screaming chicks!

© Citizenship Foundation, March 2000

SAMPLE ASSESSMENT TASKS

Written assessment tasks help pupils to be aware that there is more to moral discussion than the mere swapping of opinion. There are new concepts to be learned, and the meanings of old or familiar concepts to be refined, extended and applied in more complex situations. Formal assessment is also a useful means of reinforcing learning and assessing pupil progress, as well as evaluating the effectiveness of different teaching methods and approaches.

Certain aspects of moral education are more amenable to formal assessment than others, of course. Pupils' command of moral vocabulary, their understanding of moral concepts and the role moral concepts play in everyday judgement and debate are the most obvious candidates for this kind of assessment.

The following questions are offered as examples of the kind of assessment tasks which might be used in this way.

1. Think of some **moral** questions which might arise in a family with small children. Say why they are moral questions.

2. Describe **two** kinds of **rights**. Give an example of each kind.

3. What is the **Golden Rule**?

4. Think of another word for **justice**.

5. Think of some reasons why someone might believe **stealing** to be wrong.

6. Describe **two** kinds of **fairness**. Give an example of each kind.

7. Think of another word for **obligation**.

8. Describe **two** important differences between a **quarrel** and a **discussion**.

9. Should pupils have a say in how their schools are run? Think of some arguments both **for** and **against** this.

10. Describe **two** kinds of **duty**. Give an example of each.

11. What does it mean to say a right is an **absolute** one?

12. Think of some **moral** questions that might arise for people who work in a hospital or the health service.

13. What makes a decision a **democratic** one?

14. Think of some of the issues a person has to take into account when they have a **moral problem** to solve.

15. Speakers will sometimes use tricks of persuasion to get their listeners to accept their point of view. Think of some different kinds of **tricks of persuasion** used to do this. Give an example of each kind.

16. Write a conversation in which two people disagree about whether it is right for parents to smack their children. In your conversation try to include the following words: **fair, duty, rights, consequences**.

17. Should there be a **law** to make cyclists wear safety helmets? If this is made a law, what do you think will happen? If this is not made a law, what do you think will happen? Overall, what do you think would be for the best? Why?

18. Match the statements with the different **types of reasoning**:

A.	It is good to win, but it is not worth cheating to do it.	*1.the ends don't justify the means;*
B.	If I give you a pen, everyone else will want one and before long I'll have no pens left.	*2.the lesser of two evils;*
C.	I feel bad telling a lie, but it is better than upsetting Gran's feelings.	*3.slippery slope*